Maximize Accomplishments with Advanced Mindset Techniques

Jordi .N Anderson

All rights reserved.

Copyright © 2024 Jordi .N Anderson

Maximize Accomplishments with Advanced Mindset Techniques : Unlock Your Full Potential for Success with Proven Mindset Strategies

Funny helpful tips:

In the forest of opportunities, carve out your path with determination and vision.

Explore the world of digital currencies; cryptocurrencies and blockchain are reshaping the financial landscape.

Life advices:

In the book of existence, write chapters filled with passion, purpose, and perseverance.

Engage in regular cardiovascular check-ups; heart health is foundational to overall well-being.

Introduction

Welcome to this book, your comprehensive companion on the journey to financial empowerment and stability. In this guide, we'll navigate the intricate world of personal finance together, helping you build a secure and prosperous future.

Life's financial landscape can sometimes feel like a complex puzzle, filled with challenges and uncertainties. However, with the right tools, knowledge, and a dash of determination, you can transform your financial well-being and achieve the peace of mind you deserve.

Our approach is simple but effective: we'll take it step by step, week by week, helping you make informed decisions and take meaningful actions to reach your financial goals. Throughout this journey, you'll find action items, discussion questions, and practical advice designed to foster financial literacy and encourage wise financial choices.

In Week One, we'll start by understanding the concept of financial balance. You'll learn how to assess your current financial situation, setting the stage for a well-informed and realistic financial plan.

Week Two delves into budgeting – a key element of financial success. We'll explore expense tracking and budget purrfection (yes, purrfection, just like a cat's agility) to help you take control of your financial destiny.

Debt management takes center stage in Week Three, where we'll tackle the financial litterbox, exploring strategies to pay off debts efficiently.

Week Four shifts focus to savings and planning for the future. We'll discuss savings rates and the importance of a solid retirement plan.

Credit becomes the topic of conversation in Week Five. We'll demystify the world of credit scores and help you navigate the maze of credit-related decisions.

Week Six unveils the secrets of building wealth and securing your financial fort. We'll explore various investment options and strategies.

Are you dreaming of owning a home? Week Seven is all about turning that dream into reality. We'll discuss types of mortgages and the home-buying process, providing you with valuable insights.

Finally, we'll wrap up our financial journey by exploring the world of health insurance. You'll gain a deeper understanding of this crucial aspect of financial security.

Our goal throughout this guide is to empower you with knowledge, equip you with practical tools, and inspire you to take charge of your financial life. Remember, achieving financial success is a journey, not a destination. So, let's embark on this adventure together, paving the way for a brighter financial future. Your financial purr-spective is about to get clearer, and your financial confidence will grow stronger with each step.

Let's begin your pursuit of financial mastery!

Contents

Financial Balance 1
Week One Action Item 22
Expense Tracker 25
Discussion Questions 31
Purrfecting the Budget 34
Week Two Action Items 68
Discussion Questions 69
Debt, the Financial Litterbox 74
Purrfecting Your Loan Payoff 90
Week Three Action Items 101
Bury that Treasure 106
Week Four Action Items 120
Savings Rate 122
Retir-Purr-Ment 125
Week Five Action Items 147
Discussion Questions 148
Credit, The Great American Laser PointerChase 150
Week Six Action Items 166
Discussion Questions 167
Building Your Fort 169
Are you ready to purrchase a home? 177
Types of Mortgages 179
Steps in the Home Buying Process 181
Week Seven Action Item 185

Discussion Questions 186
Getting Under the Umbrella.. 188
Health Insurance.. 193
Discussion Questions 204
Week eight Action items.. 205
You're PAWSOME! 208
There's no trophy for money meownagement,but there should be merit badges along the way
.... 209

Financial Balance
It's not really about money

In my mid-20's, I had started a new job at a small nonprofit office. One of my coworkers, who had been there for decades, made about twice my annual salary and drove a monster high-end SUV to work. She knocked on my office door to let me know that my first paycheck would hit my account a few days later than normal, due to a bank holiday.

Without thinking about it, I quickly commented, "Okay, no problem, I'm not worried about it," and turned back to my computer. She walked away, and muttered loud enough that I could hear it, "It must be nice."

I realized two things:

1) I had committed the ultimate money taboo in the nonprofit martyrdom work world: implying that I wasn't broke.

2) I truly had zero feelings of urgency around my paycheck. Later that week, I got the paycheck deposit notification, and set about filling out my budget two months ahead. That month I saved 56% percent of my salary. Just a few years earlier, I would have handled that paycheck delay very differently (panicked).

I wasn't making much more money than when that paycheck being late would've stressed me out - I just had a different relationship with money and **better systems** in place. Instead of feeling like money was the biggest barrier in my life, money was my co-pilot. My money helped me achieve what I wanted in life - it didn't hold me back from anything.

There's so many misunderstandings about budgeting and being "good with money".

Financial balance includes having the freedom to make the choices to enjoy life. Especially if freedom includes flaming spandex.

So many people believe that being "good with money" is about counting every penny and understanding stock trades and never spending money on anything fun.

Many people think "good with money" is a trait you're born with.

The real truth is that financial *meow*nagement must be learned. Absolutely no one comes out of the womb understanding Roth IRAs.

Financial *meow*nagement is a practice - a continual process. You can't learn all this in one day and be totally set for life. To be financially well, you need to keep working on your money relationship on a regular basis.

The Consumer Financial Protection Bureau[1] did a big study of Americans to try to find the definition of financial wellness, and they discovered that feelings of financial wellness correlate to a few different factors:

- Control over day-to-day, month-to-month finances
- Capacity to absorb a financial shock
- Financial freedom to make choices to enjoy life
- On track to meet financial goals

Notice that none of these qualifications for financial well-being involve your income. They *do* require you to manage your money, consider your values, set goals for yourself, and live below your means. While making more money, or having more money, can help with your financial wellness (and very much might be part of your long-term money plan) - you can be financially well without having a high net worth, a trust fund, or a six-figure salary.

Your financial well being is not your income.

Many people - at all income levels - convince themselves that if they just had some magic amount of money (more than they have now), all their problems would be gone. It's like how my cat is convinced that whatever is on the other side of the locked door is the most important thing to her happiness - but when I open the door, she reconsiders and realizes that she could've taken the same nap on either side of the door.

Making more money, especially if you are living close to the poverty level, can definitely help your financial wellness. I'm not denying the power of "more money." But no matter how much money you make, if you don't fix your relationship with money, you'll never really get out of the financial litterbox. You'll just create even bigger money problems for yourself. And a modest income with good money choices CAN make all the difference.

Influences on Financial Well-Being[2]

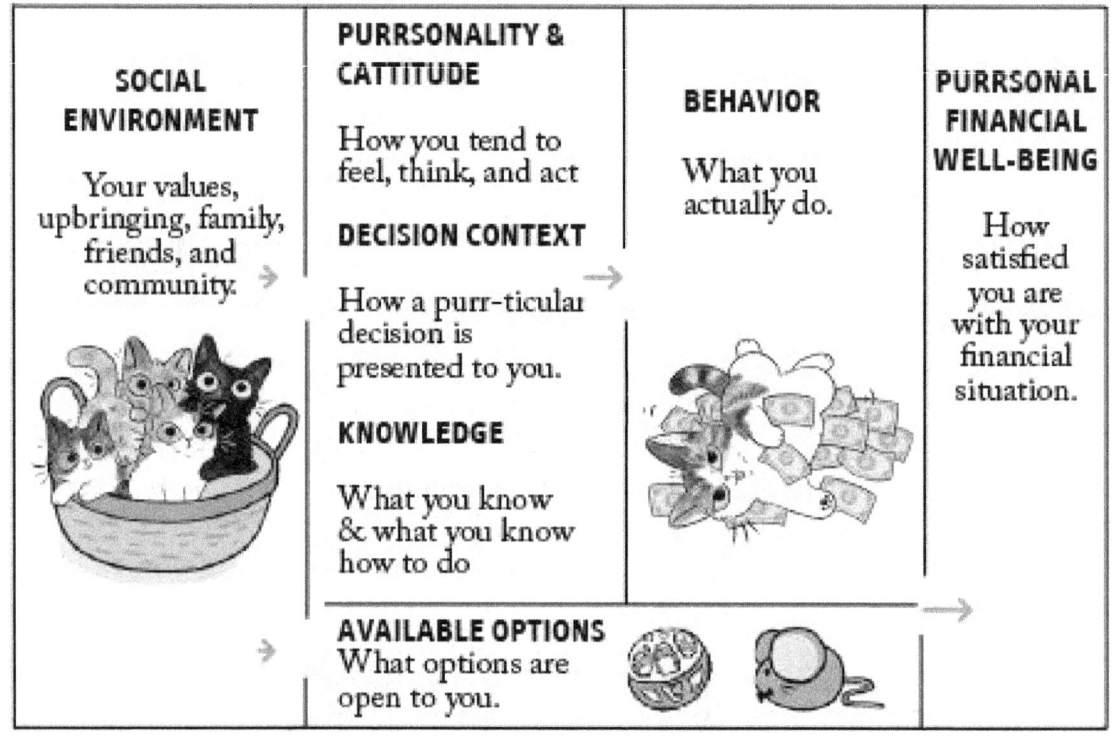

Start with what is in your control

At any given time, some factors of your financial well-being are outside your own control, and some are in your control. Understanding the dif*fur*rence is part of getting a handle on your money.

Your social environment and upbringing is one factor in your financial well-being. *Purr*haps your family was able to pay for your education. Or maybe you have large amounts of student loans because your family couldn't afford to finance it. Both are examples of factors outside your control that can significantly impact your financial well-being.

Even the way you're presented with financial decisions matters - we call this decision context. For example, you might have been automatically added to a retirement plan at work and didn't need to think about saving. Or *purr*haps your employer requires you to have the knowledge to opt-in to the retirement plan.

But the good news is that these factors outside your control don't write your whole money story - your financial behavior is also guided by your own *purr*sonality, attitudes, knowledge, and skills. (And you're reading this book, so you're helping fix the knowledge part!)

There's certain things about money that will always be outside your control - but *how you choose to live your life*, within the options available to you, helps create your level of financial well-being. If you act like nothing is within your own control, you will never get ahead. **You do have the potential to change your financial future, with some flexibility, planning, and grit.**

If you don't feel good about being in the financial litterbox, you can change things - at any point in your life. And the good news is that numbers are the smallest part of the total equation - most of money is emotional and behavioral.

To create real change, you need to start this process from your values. If you feel like you're fighting yourself with a budget, you're never going to love it.

If you pick financial goals out of a hat, you won't feel good when you accomplish them. But if you start with the foundation of your values, your goals as a person, you're going to start LOVING financial *meow*nagement because it gives you the freedom to go after the things in your life that you care about.

All of us are carrying around internal scripts about how we relate to money, and the weight of these scripts - these unspoken beliefs that we absorbed from our social environment - can often be the biggest hangup to getting a handle on our money.

Money Scripts

There are plenty of unspoken scripts about money we carry around from our upbringing, our families, and our community. These scripts shape our money behavior in ways that aren't always clear at first. Do you recognize yourself in any of these statements?

Circle any you identify with.

Spending money makes me feel ill.

It bothers me when I discover I could have gotten the same thing elsewhere for less money.

I make most of my financial decisions out of fear.

When I was a child, money seemed to be the most important thing in life.

Money controls the things I do and don't do in life.

The adults in my life hid spending from one another.

I will always be in debt; it's just a fact of life.

I feel like having wealth or money is based on luck.

Someone has used access to money to control my decisions.

I don't believe I will ever have enough money to retire.

When I was growing up, the adults in my life told me that a hypothetical payday (like winning the lottery) would solve all our problems.

I think people who are wealthy must have done something morally wrong to get there.

"We can't afford it" was something I heard a lot growing up.

Money is just a tool

A common money myth that many of us carry around is that money is evil. But **money is just a tool** that helps you accomplish your goals. Money can be used to accomplish bad things, sure, but it can also be used to accomplish good things. It is similar to a brick - a brick can be used to harm a litter of kittens or it could be used to build a new cat cafe. Money - like a brick - is neutral, it's how you use it that matters. Money can be used to make art, to feed hungry people, to grow catnip, to clean water, to make dangling stick toys for bored kittens, to build houses.

If you believe that having money is immoral, you're going to have trouble getting your finances in order. It wasn't until I worked to shed my belief that I needed to live in poverty to help those in poverty that I started to get my head above financial water. Getting my money together was the key to having the time and freedom to support community projects I always wanted to do, like fostering cats - and I didn't suddenly become a bad person just because I opened a retirement account.

Your money is a reflection of your values

You can see what a person truly values if you look at their bank statement and their calendar. What do they make time for? Where do their money and time really go?

If you were to review your bank statement for the past couple months, what would you find about your values - are you prioritizing the things you say you value? Are you spending your money in places that don't help you towards your ultimate goals?

I know if you feel that you're barely making it until the next payday, ultimate goals can feel like a silly indulgence. In that case, maybe your first values-based goal is to break the paycheck-to-paycheck cycle - because you value security, your family, and want to contribute to something larger than you are right *meow*.

Don't get caught up in feeling like you must have the "right" financial goals. I have found that diving into setting financial goals without laying this unmissable foundation of your values is a recipe for burnout. If you feel like you're chasing a hard goal like paying off debt, saving up an emergency fund, or buying a house without identifying what drives you, you're setting yourself up to fail.

I'm a pretty rational person who doesn't engage with magical thinking nonsense - but the data doesn't lie. **People who set goals based on their values are more likely to meet those goals.** This seemingly self-indulgent exercise of thinking about your goals and your values is not something you can ignore. This is a crucial step for success on this financial well-being journey.

Values

Values are a quality or standard that you consider worthwhile. Circle any that stand out to you, or add your own ideas in the blank space. And remember, it's okay if you're not positive these are "right" - they can change, you can revisit them. That is OKAY.

INDEPENDENCE	RECREATION	FAITH
SAFETY	JUSTICE	SECURITY
LEISURE	EQUALITY	ADVENTURE
FAMILY	CREATIVITY	BEAUTY
STABILITY	KNOWLEDGE	
COMMUNITY	FRIENDSHIP	
CHARITY	FREEDOM	

BUILDING THE FOUNDATION

MY NAME IS _____

I am a (circle any that apply)

       MAKER DOER LOVER FIGHTER
       SURVIVOR CREATOR THINKER

IN THE PAST, I HAVE LET MY RELATIONSHIP WITH MONEY _____
_____
_____

BUT NOW I'M READY TO _____
_____
_____

EXAMPLE

> I AM AFRAID THAT IF I START BUDGETING, I HAVE FAILED AS AN ADULT BECAUSE I THINK LIVING ON A BUDGET IS ALL ABOUT DEPRIVATION.

I AM AFRAID _____
_____ BECAUSE _____
_____
_____
_____
_____
_____

I AM SAYING YES TO:
NAPS

I AM SAYING NO TO:
FLEAS

I WANT TO UNDO THE HARMFUL MONEY SCRIPT OF _____

___ BECAUSE _____

EXAMPLE

> I WANT TO UNDO THE HARMFUL MONEY SCRIPT OF I THINK THAT BEING RICH MAKES YOU IMMORAL BECAUSE I DON'T WANT TO FEEL BAD ABOUT MAKING ENOUGH TO PROVIDE FOR MY FAMILY.

Digging up your values

When I heard the word "values", I immediately think back to bland posters on the wall of the breakroom at my first grocery store job. While identifying your values can seem like a corporate retreat-style distraction from Important Money Decisions, it's actually essential to figuring out your next step in fiscal *meow*nagement. This worksheet can help you identify some values.

PEOPLE DESCRIBE ME AS

- _____
- _____
- _____

- _____
- _____
- _____

I'M HAPPIEST WHEN I AM:

- With my loved ones
- Making something new
- Experiencing a new thing
- Cuddling my cats
- Doing an a skilled activity

I'M HAPPIEST AROUND PEOPLE:

- Who teach me new things
- Who encourage me
- Who are relaxed
- Who are adventurous
- Who challenge me

IF IT WERE TOTALLY UP TO ME, I WOULD SPEND MY DAYS DOING:

- _____
- _____
- _____

- _____
- _____
- _____

I WANT TO BE REMEMBERED FOR THESE QUALITIES:

- _____
- _____
- _____

- _____
- _____
- _____

Goal ideas

Use this space - get messy - to fill in some ideas about what you hope to accomplish in the next 5 years. These aren't set in stone, you're not committing to them. Don't limit yourself to financial goals. What do you want to be remembered for? Think about the values you've identified. If you're struggling to come up with ideas, look back at what you want to be remembered for, and when and where you're happiest.

Accelerate your timeline

Imagine you find out that you only have 10 years to live. Your doctor says you'll never feel sick but you'll have no advance notice of the moment of your death. Your finances are exactly the same as they are today. What would you change about your lifestyle? What would you change about your finances?

You may notice that your financial goals change in this scenario. Some folks, for example, might be inspired to buckle down and pay off their mortgage because they want their partner or kids to have a mortgage-free house. Or they might immediately start working only 30 hours a week because they no longer need to save for retirement and they want more time to make art. Thinking about this scenario can help you dig up some of your core values.

Now, Let's turn those into financial goals!

We're going to work to identify your top financial goal, and the core values behind it. If you can't come up with a financial goal, think about the financial resources you need to accomplish what you want to be remembered for.

Here are some examples of value-based financial goals:

Stability: Saving for a down payment for a home

Community: Contribute financially to strangers in need
Education: Save to pay for your child's college in full
Charity: Giving a percentage of your income to causes you care about
Creativity: Pay off debt so that you can have more resources for art
Family: Saving to take time off to raise children
Independence: Have enough of a buffer to live alone
Security: Building a 6-month emergency fund
Leisure: Saving up for a sabbatical or vacation

Week One Action Item
Get tracking

The first step in budgeting isn't even setting up a budget. It's tracking what you spend for a week. Deceptively simple, this is also one of the hardest activities for many folks. To do this exercise, I don't want you to edit or change what you spend - spend as you normally do - but just track it. (That turns out to be harder than you expect.)

I recommend doing this on paper at first - even if you feel like a bit of a silly kitten pulling out a sheet of paper at the counter at the coffee shop. Feel free to tear the page out of this book to carry around - make a mess! It's okay. Money can get messy. Getting control of your money shouldn't be embarrassing!

The reason I recommend using paper to write down expenses at first is that while eventually it's likely you'll use an app or something slightly more sophisticated than a folded sheet of paper, I don't want you to get caught in a hole doing research, trying to find the perfect app and learn a new system. What I want you to do to is simply track your expenses. Just write down everything that comes out of your pockets and your account.

Some people ask me if they should track their automatic payments for rent or student loans, or if they should track pocket change. The answer is YES to everything. You should track absolutely everything you spend - any money that goes to anyone else - over the course of a week. Because it's easy to hide spending from yourself if you create restrictions ("I'll only track the cash account, not the credit card because I'll look that up later," you say to yourself, only to realize you definitely did not do that.)

This exercise is all about building a habit - it's about behavioral change. This exercise is trying to help you recognize when you spend money. This is *not* about shame. This exercise is not meant to make you feel terrible every time you pull out your wallet. It's simply about building a habit. Because those tiny purchases - that coffee, that burrito for lunch, that interest fee you paid because you forgot the due date - those add up over time.

So I want you to track your purchases for a week. And do it on paper (there's a tracker you can use on page 27) without getting too caught up in the mechanics of it. If you forget the paper, try to remember before you go to bed every night to enter the purchases before you fall asleep. Set a reminder on your phone or a post-it note next to your bed.

Even if you hate this exercise - remember it's just for a week. You can live with carrying around a sheet of paper and pen for a week. I guarantee it. You won't die from death by paper cuts and financial accountability.

Here's what I don't want you to do: forget to track your expenses, and then try to catch up using your bank account statement at the end of the week. That's not behavior change. That's not building a habit - that's procrastinating on your money and then trying to "catch up". If you find yourself doing that, I want you to start the week over, carry around that sheet of paper, and start again.

There is nothing magical about the 1st of the month, Sunday or Monday. You can make the choice to start handling your money anytime.

Here's the trick to this exercise. The last column of the expense tracker on the next page has a smiley face. I want you to rate how each purchase made you feel - a smiley face or a frowny face. This might seem simplistic, but just give it a shot.

Over time, we want our monetary exchanges to be better planned - and be in accordance with our values. That means when you look back at what you've spent, you don't feel slightly sick, but instead feel really excited about how much closer you're getting to your big goals.

It's never going to be *purr*fect - it's likely you won't love paying your electric bill or your internet bill - but you may recognize how awesome it is to have lights and cat videos available at 3AM.

Expense Tracker

How to use: Every time you make a purchase this week, enter it on the expense tracker and choose an appropriate category (groceries or restaurants). Use the last column to rate how each purchase made you feel - good or bad? Then add up all your purchases by category on page 29.

DATE	DESCRIPTION	CATEGORY	AMOUNT	:) / :(

DATE	DESCRIPTION	CATEGORY	AMOUNT	:) / :(

CATEGORIES

CATEGORY	DAY 1	DAY 2	DAY 3	DAY 4	DAY 5	DAY 6	DAY 7	WEEK TOTAL
RENT/MORTGAGE								
UTILITIES								
TRANSPORT								
GROCERIES								
DINING OUT								
COFFEE								
ALCOHOL								
TOBACCO								
MEDICAL								
CLOTHING								
GROOMING								
GIFTS								
EDUCATION								
CHILDCARE								
PET CARE								
PHONE								
INTERNET								
TV								
INSURANCE								
SAVINGS								
DEBT								

Discussion Questions

*These discussion questions are great if you are going through **A Cat's Guide to Money** with friends - but they're also worth having the conversation with yourself, your accountability partner, or just writing them out below.*

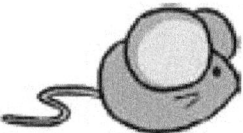

Why are values such an important part of a financial plan? What do you think is the risk if you craft a financial plan without considering your values?

You learned in this lesson that financial well-being is not net worth or salary. Why is that? What does achieving financial wellness mean to your every day life?

Consider the signs of financial imbalance below:

- *Making only minimum payments on debt*
- *No plans for financial future*
- *No savings plan*
- *No assets (except vehicle)*
- *Waiting to pay bills until payday*

- *Scared to look at bank account balance*
- *Can't afford even a short time off work*
- *Frequently worry about money*

Do you see some of those traits in yourself? Which of those warning signs do you most want to improve on?

Purrfecting the Budget
Building a system for your money

It's time. We're going to talk about the budget.

Now, I know that many people think that budget is a scary word - they feel like "living on a budget" implies extreme frugality, being broke, or some sort of deprivation. "Budget" as a word gets a bad rap. But for most folks, a budget is the #1 key to getting control of their money.

A budget doesn't have to be rigid and it doesn't have to involve endless spreadsheets. It doesn't need to be monthly. A budget doesn't mean you never get to drink fancy coffee or go out for cocktails again.

Following a budget doesn't even mean, necessarily, that **you need to change your spending behavior at all from what it is now**. If you're comfortable with your level of spending and savings then a budget might simply be a long-term plan for you and a check-in on how you're progressing towards your goals. It's not meant to be a tool to make you miserable, but instead help you feel in control of your money.

Maybe you feel like that you're doing pretty good with money - you've optimized your expenses, you always have enough in your accounts to cover an unexpected expense, and you've paid down your student loans.

But at the same time, maybe you can't exactly tell me how much you spent last month on restaurants. Or you went on a vacation last year, but you're not sure how much you spent total on the trip. You're fine with that because you're making decent money and you always have enough to provide for yourself.

But I want you to imagine that by budgeting, you found an extra $75 a month. You realized that you're overpaying for internet or that you really could forgo that gym membership you don't use.

If you invested that extra $75 a month - which before taxes is actually about $100 a month- into your retirement - from age 30 until age 65, you'd have a cool half million dollars in your retirement account based on the average rate of return (more on that in the Retire*purr*ment chapter)[3]

EXPENSE	TODAY	OVER 10 YEARS	OVER 30 YEARS
Fancy Coffee	$4 a day	$22,289	$190,453
Smoking	$35 a week	$26,857	$222,233
Lunch at work	$8 a day, 5 days a week	$29,273	$238,468
Weekly happy hour	$25 a week	$18,661	$158,731

I don't know about you, but if all I had to was trim out $75 a month out of my budget by spending 20 minutes on the phone with Big Evil Internet Corporation to be a half-millionaire at retirement age, I'd jump all over that deal.

Some people feel like a budget will close in on them and make life not fun anymore. Or they feel that budgeting doesn't work for them because they have ADD or are bad at math or they're simply not "built that way."

But here's the reality: budgeting is essential. Budgeting is part of two of the four keystones to financial well-being - "control over day-to-day, month-to-month finances" and "on track to meeting financial goals."

And you can find a way to make budgeting work for you. There are many flavors and methods of budgeting, for all sorts of brains and lifestyles. The practice of actively engaging with your money and crafting a plan is the basic foundation of financial well-being - and it looks a little different for everyone.

David Wisconsin
Urban Homesteader, Bunny Raiser & Homeschooling Dad

What a budget isn't

A budget doesn't mean you can never order takeout again. That's the totally wrong view of a budget. A budget gives you permission - it gives you a plan. It just means that you have a "takeout" line item in your budget and you feel great that you know you can meet your other obligations despite having springrolls and Hot & Sour soup for dinner. No one else cares *how* you spend your money in the budget - you just need to know that you have a plan for it. A budget gives you the ability to pull out your wallet with confidence, knowing you're on track for your Big Goals despite having indulgences and fun.

A budget **lets you live a truer reflection of your values.** Budgeting is a practice, not a theory. It brings those dream cloud exercises that we did in chapter one on your values and your goals into your every day life. Setting up a budget for yourself and using it on a regular basis helps you see if your life is passing the "bank statement test" - does your bank statement actually reflect what you truly value in life?

You're not going to feel confident about your money by being passive about it.

I'm not asking you to obsess over every single detail if that doesn't work for your brain and personality, but I am asking you to *participate in your money*. If you've got money coming in the door and going out the door, I want you to have a conversation with yourself - and your partner or co-parent, if you have one - about that money before it walks right back out the door.

If your household income is $35,000 a year, which would be about $17.50 per hour, you're going to have half a million dollars pass through your hands in the next 15 years of your life. That's a lot of money to handle without making a plan for it, and it only scales up as your income goes up.

I've heard people tell me their income is too high for a budget - especially folks making six-figure salaries when working in high-demand fields. "I don't need a budget because I make good money. Budgets are for broke people, I can spend whatever I want because I make $150,000 a year."

If you are making an excellent income, there's even more reason for you to have a plan for your money - that amount of money coming in means that you could accomplish some really big goals, if only you had a plan for your money. You could be endowing a fund for the arts, a new cat shelter, or scholarship for youth from your hometown. You could acquire a sailboat and sail around the world, taking off from work for years. You could be investing in promising new companies. You could have a mortgage-free home in just a few short years, perhaps allowing you to work a part-time schedule to raise children. You could self-fund a run for office. You could be retired in your early 30's on that kind of income, if only you had a plan for your money and stuck with it.

Do you really want to avoid making a plan for your money just because you don't like the word budget?

If you have a budget, you can avoid the lifestyle inflation trap that so many higher-income individuals fall into: they believe the money will continue forever and they spend it before they earn it. They go into debt buying things and experiences to "keep up" with their high-income, debt-ridden coworkers and friends (expensive housing, cars, vacations, clothing, technology, club memberships).

They never amass any wealth or think about their long-term goals, and if the high income dries up, they're broke without a back up plan.

At all income levels, if you sit down and think about where you really want your money to go, instead of mindlessly buying what society tells you that you *should have,* you will be much more financially well. And, frankly, happier. Money itself can't make you happy - but if you are using your money in a way that's based on your values and goals, you're likely to be a lot happier. My cat, Dora, is much happier when she's working towards her goals of running around the apartment full-speed rather than the societally-imposed standards of being quiet at 3AM.

Remember, money is a tool - you might as well put it to work for you.

So the key to all of this - the building a financial plan rooted in your own goals - is the budget. If the word budget brings up bad feelings for you, let's try spending plan. Written plan. Money minder. Cash flow system. Money-fantastic-glitter-outline.

Whatever works for you. But the key to the budget is to find a system that works for you, and actually put it into practice. Because, honestly, if you're 99% of people, you are not going to be *paw*some at money by accident. It just doesn't happen.

You Do You: Values And budgeting

My budget is not your budget. And while you think this has to do with income and expenses, the secret is that budgets have less to do with money and more to do with values. Remember, money is a medium of exchange of value.

Awhile back, I had a friend find out that I was researching a new gym. I mentioned I was interested in a MegaGym – partially for the hot tub – and he said "wow, I heard MegaGym was really expensive." Initially I was shocked, because at $39 a month, it was the cheapest gym I was considering.

For the past year, I had been spending $79 a month on membership which allowed me to go to high-end fitness classes all over the city – so half of that expense sounds like a deal to me. I'm a former competitive athlete and coach, so fitness is really important to me.

Now this isn't to sell you on the idea that an expensive gym membership is important for you. I'm not here to inflate your budget unnecessarily. This is to show you that **my budget is completely different from my friend's budget**.

A regular fitness program is part of my values – I value my health and I value the community aspects of a small fitness studio. When it comes to fitness, I know what works for me and I'm willing to pay for quality. I have made the choice to make my budget reflect my values. I am willing to spend a little less in other areas – rarely dining out, not drinking alcohol, not owning a car - in order to splurge on the things that reflect my own values.

My friend spends $10 a month at a discount gym out in his neighborhood and gets a perfectly fine workout. But he also chooses to live in a smaller community that is far enough from his job that he spends 1.5 hours a day commuting in a car. This is a choice he's made because he wants a certain kind of home for his family. His values of family and community have led him to a different budget: he wants to live in a smaller community for his children and he wants to have a larger house for his hobby projects and his family.

Both my friend and I make tradeoffs in our budget. He's willing to drive and own a car - I am not. I choose to live close to my job and share a small apartment, which means I don't need to own a car. The average American car payment is $550 per month[4] – I am happy to allocate my dollars elsewhere.

While my friend was floored by my $80 per month on fitness classes, I wouldn't want to spend every day commuting in a car. This isn't a value judgment on either of us; this is about what we each want to get out of our money to reflect our values. The very core tenet of budgeting is "you do you".

What you're going to learn as you start budgeting is that no one else can budget for you. Following someone else's money plan won't make you happy if it doesn't have your goals and your values as the foundation. If you want to spend your money on sparkly unitards and platform boots but cut back on the amount you spend on entertainment, dining out, or groceries, that's okay.

There is literally no such thing as a perfect budget. My budget might make you feel deprived in some areas and wasteful in others. Money is an exchange of value, and for you to really rock your budget, you need to actually think about your values. You do you.

**Kitty Starbudget would like to remind you that it is OK to budget for platform boots and glitter if that's your jam.
You do you.**

So how do you get your values into the budget?

Engineering your "values" into the budget can seem like a magic trick - especially when you're just trying to make ends meet. But it's just as simple as asking yourself "Why?" when you allocate money into a category. "Why do I care about this?" or "Why do I want to do that?" Keep repeating

"Why?" like an annoying 3-year-old as you're looking over your expenses, and the final answer will help reveal a value.

You can get creative if you've identified a value but don't see it reflected in your budget. You can add in budget categories that will encourage you to do more of the things that represent your values. This could be explicit or implicit. Perhaps you want to see more movies with your family because of your value of *family* and you figure that $10 a month for a Moviepass will force you to go to the movies more than twice a month – that's an explicit link.

But maybe you want to start volunteering at the local animal shelter every week to support your values of *community* and *loving on kitties,* but you know that you need to budget for a latte every week on the way there to get yourself motivated to go to the far-flung suburban shelter – that's an implicit budget connection.

Gizmo's core values include naps and he's using his money to facilitate that value.

Making the budget

Hopefully you're convinced that a budget can be a wonderful tool for feeling better about your money and taking control of your financial future.

Now it's time for our action plan. I want this to be easy to set up for you. Since you've tracked your expenses for seven days already (week one action item on page 27), all you need to do is to add up all your expenses into the category sheet on page 29.

Then, take each category and multiple by four to fill in a rough draft of the monthly "Kitten Budget" on page 50. (I call it a Kitten Budget because it's small and easy to look at.) If this is sounding like a lot of math, grab your phone calculator. Don't make this too hard on yourself!

Looking at your Kitten Budget, you'll realize that it's missing some things - perhaps your rent, your student loan payments, your monthly medication expenses. Time to fill those categories in.

You can sit down with your accountability partner or significant other or yourself and a cup of your favorite beverage and put this together in an evening. Just like with tracking expenses, I recommend doing it on paper for at least one month - before you dive into learning a new app or platform.

It's never exactly the same

Now, I will tell you that every single person that has done the week one exercise of tracking their expenses has told me that the week that they tracked was exceptional and out of the ordinary. Here's the thing you'll learn as you get into the groove with budgeting: no month is the same when it comes to money. There's always something - someone's birthday, an unexpected bill, your washing machine falls apart or you're traveling or your kid gets sick, which is why you need to build in planning for unexpected in your budget and learn to roll with the punches.

Known Unknowns

The next goal is to plan for your less frequent expenses with sinking funds. You can use sinking funds for infrequent expenses like annual fees, property tax, and insurance - for example, if you pay $240 annually for renter's insurance, you would save $240/12 months or $20 per month into your renter's insurance category. This means that you won't be surprised and "robbing" other categories for the money when the expense comes up.

Sinking funds don't necessarily need to be their own bank accounts - in my case, I simply designate the money in my budget, but leave it to pile up in my checking account. However, if you have impulse control struggles, putting your sinking funds into a separate (harder to find) account can be a smart way to "trick" yourself into forgetting the money is there.

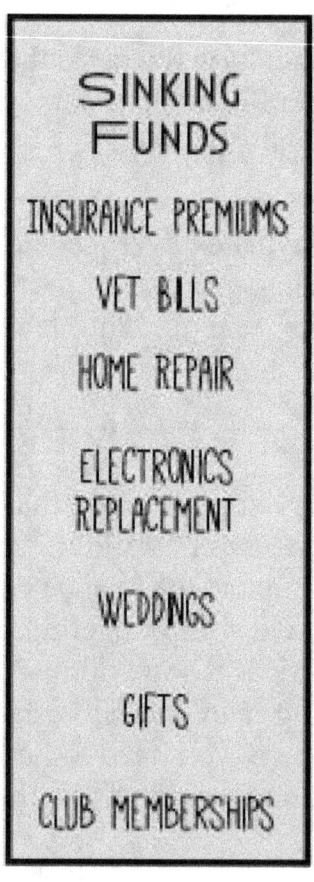

Sinking funds are also very useful for the "known unknowns" in your budget - things that you know will happen in the future but you don't know when - like fixing the car, the water heater, buying new glasses, or replacing your phone. Sinking funds help you plan for future uncertainty.

Sinking funds help you avoid the alternative: panickedly delaying your rent or borrowing money in order to pay off a big insurance bill or replace a laptop you need for work. Or having to turn down paying work because you don't have a functional car. Think about big known unknowns in your life and create sinking funds for them.

Savings

Once you've filled in that budget, let me ask, did you remember to save anything? Because the first rule of budgeting is to pay yourself first. No one else is going to save for you, so it's your responsibility to pay yourself before you pay others. Other people and companies are always going to want to get your money, but you're never going to get ahead if you don't see yourself as your first financial *purr*iority.

So put aside a bit of savings for yourself *right meow*. Even if it's just $10 per month.

The key here is to break the "normal" money habit of paying everyone else before you pay yourself. That's why savings is right at the top of the Kitten

Budget. We'll cover savings more in-depth in chapter four, but get started with at least $1 now.

Living within your means

Now that you've got savings and expenses and "known unknowns" accounted for, here's the important part - the money coming in has to match what is going out. Otherwise you're living beyond your means. If it's really not adding up - the amount you have coming in every month is less than your expenses, you need to either increase your income or cut out some expenses. Like many things in this book, this is simple, but not easy.

It's really going to suck at first

So, real talk. I truly believe budgeting is awesome. But it's gonna suck for the first couple months. It really will. You'll forget that your auto insurance comes due every 6 months or that subscription you signed up for or that there's school fees to pay. You'll probably be totally off in your estimates in at least one category.

That is OK - this is a learning process. Hopefully you'll find a budgeting system that you'll be able, in some form, to use *for the rest of your life* - so it's okay if it takes a couple months to get used to it.

If you've watched a 5-week-old kitten try to hunt a toy, you've seen that while adorable, baby kittens suck at hunting in the beginning. They fall over. Their aim is terrible. They give up and take naps 2 minutes into playing. But if they keep doing it, they get better. And eventually they can fully decimate a catnip toy in seconds.

The second month you start budgeting, it's going to get a little bit easier. Like the kitten, your practice has improved your aim. You've gotten better at guessing how much you spend on groceries each week. You figured out you need to plan for movie dates and co-pays. But there's still some unexpected things in the budget.

The third month is usually the point at which it really starts to click for most people. You'll start rolling. You start to feel that you have a great handle on your relationship with money. You are a fierce hunter kitten, ready to vanquish all of the hair ties.

You might have to change up the way you budget a few times to find something that works for you. The next page has different kinds of money tactics and budgeting methods based on *purr*sonality types.

Getting started with budgeting is a lot to pack in so feel free to review this chapter - come back to it, give things a fresh start whenever you need. Remember, financial *meow*nagement must be learned - but it also must be practiced. This is a long-term shift in the way you think.

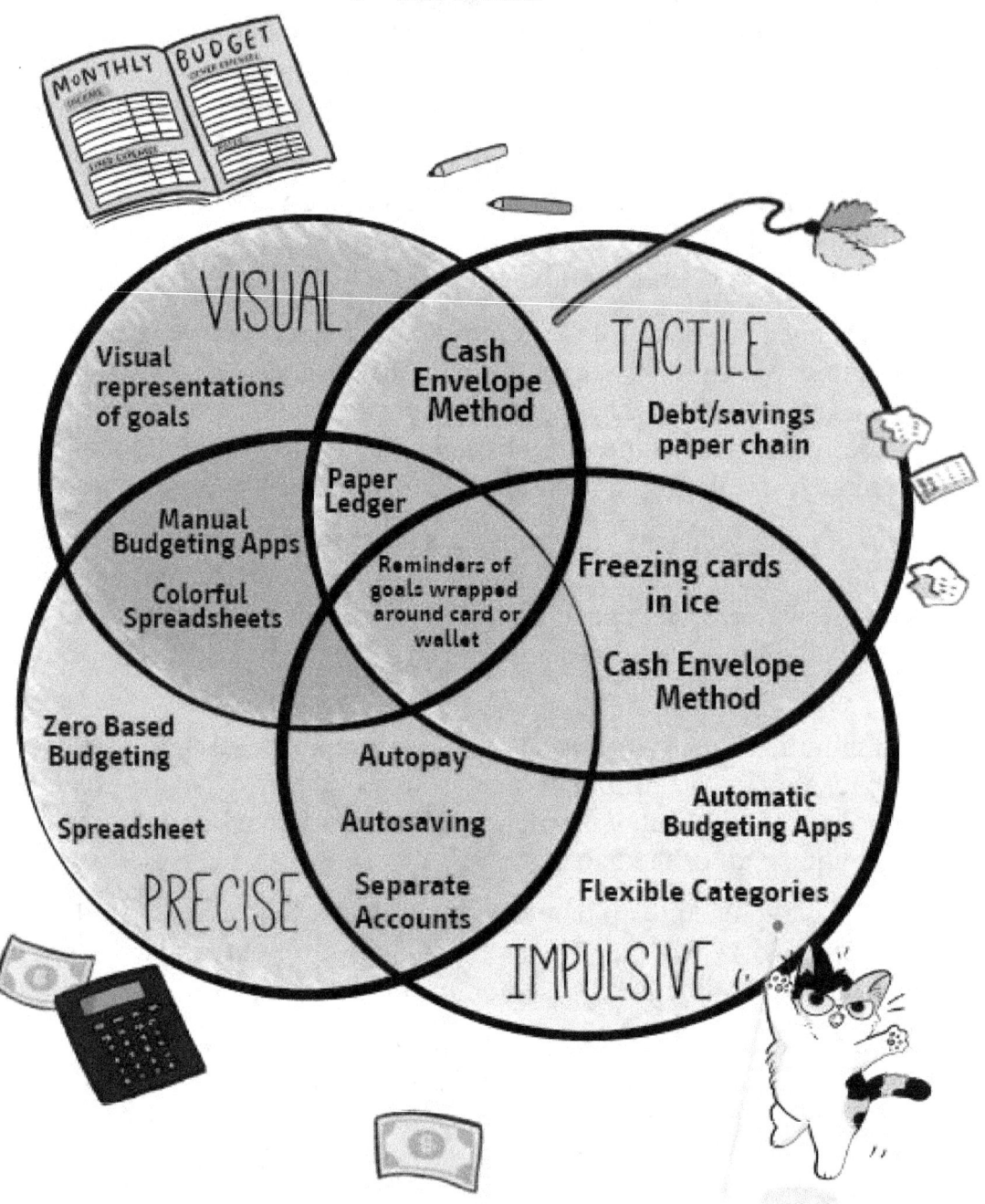

You can find a budgeting method that works for you!

There are many different budgeting tactics, techniques, and methodologies. You're free to mix and match methods. None of these are "right" or "wrong"- whatever works for you is the best! You can add or subtract any of these techniques with the Kitten Budget.

Automatic Budgeting App If precise data doesn't matter to you, an automatic budgeting app that links to your accounts will give you an overview of your spending from a bird's eye view and help keep you on track without a ton of daily effort.

Autopay Set your bills on autopay so you never miss another one. Many banks will even mail checks automatically for you to folks that won't take a card (like landlords).

Autosaving Set automatic transfers into your savings and retirement - many employers will even do this directly from your paycheck, so you never even "see" the money.

Cash Envelope Method Place all your spending money in envelopes (or binder clips or clear jars) designated by category, and only spend from that envelope. If you run out of money in one envelope, you'll need to stop spending entirely for that category and pull cash from another (make sure you're not stealing from rent to cover concerts!) You can do this for all your expenses or just discretionary categories.

Colorful Spreadsheets Add colors to your spreadsheets to help keep you focused. I hate seeing "red" overspent!

Debt/Savings Chain Make a daisy chain out of paper like it's kindergarten and pull one off everytime you add to savings or pay off debt (one chain link per $100?)

Flexible Categories The bigger your categories, the easier it is to move things around (a common percentage: 50% needs/30% wants/20% savings).

You can even try separate accounts!

Freezing Cards in Ice If impulse spending is problematic, freeze your debit or credit cards inside a block of ice. You'll have to wait for the ice to melt before you can spend! (Delete the numbers out of your browser auto-fill memory, too!)

Manual Budgeting App An application that requires entering transactions "manually" (by upload or data entry) is a great fit for those that love data and control.

Paper Ledger Using a checkbook register or a nice thick paper ledger like our grandmother might have used can help make the budget feel "real".

Separate Accounts Set your money on autopilot and prevent overspending by auto-depositing your money into separate accounts for savings, discretionary, and bills.

Spreadsheet This budgeting classic is excellent for folks that love precise data. Every spreadsheet program has a personal budget template you can adapt to your liking.

Visual Representation of Goals Some folks need to see their money goals in front of them to stay focused. Try a vision board, collage, bullet journal, coloring sheet (with blocks for savings) or sticky note art to remind yourself of your goals. Try **wrapping it around your card or wallet** so you see it every time you spend money.

Zero Based Budget A budgeting method where every single dollar is given a job, down to the last cent, and the goal is to be left with $0 unbudgeted. Even savings has a "job"- this way you know exactly where everything is going.

Kitten Budget

It is time to get you started budgeting! Over the long-term, your budgeting will become more precise, but this worksheet is meant to get you rolling quickly.

INCOME	BUDGET
Monthly Income (before taxes)	
Taxes + Other Deductions (Union Fees, Etc)	
Pre-Tax Retirement Contributions	
Total Take Home Pay	

SAVINGS	BUDGET
Emergency Fund	
Post-Tax Retirement	
TOTAL A	

HOUSEHOLD	BUDGET
Rent/Mortgage	
Household Goods	
Renter's/Homeowner's Insurance	
Furniture	
Taxes & HOA	
Repairs & Maintenance	
TOTAL B	

UTILITIES	BUDGET
Electricity	
Water/Sewer	
Gas	
Phone	
Internet	
Garbage/Recycling	
TOTAL C	

FOOD & DRINK	BUDGET
Groceries	
Dining Out	
Alcohol & Coffee	
TOTAL D	

TRANSPORTATION	BUDGET
Car Payment	
Gas & Oil	
Auto Insurance	
Transit	
Repairs & Maintenance	
TOTAL E	

HEALTH	BUDGET
Health Insurance	
Co-pays	
Gym Fees	
Health Savings Account	
TOTAL F	

Total from All Categories A-G	

OTHER EXPENSES	BUDGET
Charity	
Clothing	
Childcare	
Gifts	
Educational Expenses	
Travel	
Entertainment	
Life/Disability Insurance	
Cable/Netflix/Spotify	
Sinking Funds	
Debt (from below)	
Pets	
Other	
Other	
TOTAL G	

THIS IS YOUR BASELINE MONTHLY BUDGET — IF IT'S LESS THAN YOUR TAKE HOME PAY, CONGRATS!

DEBT	MINIMUM PAYMENT (I)	EXTRA PAYMENT (II)	TOTAL PAYMENT (I + II)
TOTAL			

BUDGET BUSTERS

Do you know the difference between your "needs" and your "wants"? You get constantly bombarded with information about what you "need" from advertisers, friends, family members. You're surrounded by billboards telling you that you can't live without a vacation, food delivered to your home, and a new car. In fact, we're relatively simple humans to operate, and you probably don't need tropical vacations, margaritas after work, seat warmers, or someone to pre-chop your vegetables for you. If you want those things, that is fine - as long as they are a reasonable expense in your budget.

But if you're faced with a BIG task of paying off debt or saving for a Big Goal, consider using the budget to re-evaluate what is *a real need vs a want* - in some categories, you can try cutting the expense for a few months as a trial.

Cable: With the plethora of low-cost streaming services out there, you probably don't need 300 channels.

Dining Out: Those happy hours and appetizers add up quickly. Perhaps you can try a 2 week break from eating out and see that you don't explode. Learn to love your kitchen again?

Subscription Box Services: Do you really need a box filled with mystery items showing up at your door every month? You're paying for something you don't even know if you value! Does your cat really need more cute collars and catnip mice every single month?

App Subscriptions: When you start looking at your budget, you may notice you're being charged for apps and software you don't even use. Get that money back!

Travel: Oh, I know those Instagram photos look awesome. But if you're focusing on paying off debt, you can likely put off the travel for a couple years while you knock out your debt.

Car Payment: The average car payment is $509/month - think what could happen if you were saving that money each month instead. Consider selling and buying a modest car in cash if you feel like the car is drowning your budget. (Or go by bike or transit!)

Every single person who has accomplished great things in Get Your Money Together - paying off tons of debt, saving like a maniac, or just feeling at peace with their money - has said the budget is the key. So this chapter is more important than everything else. I don't care your income level - high or low or in the middle - you need a budget. So spend as much time as you need with this.

You won't regret starting budgeting.

Emotional Spending

You know how cats spend most of the day lounging, taking naps and two hour baths, but then at random points in the day they catch the "zoomies" and suddenly start running at startling speeds between furniture objects? (My cat prefers to do this at whatever time humans are sleeping.) Well, spending can be kind of like that.

**Salespeople and advertisers try to trigger your emotions to encourage you buy things.
Just as Cider is trying to play with your emotions with his adorable face to get treats.**

After starting to budget and track your expenses, you may discover you do a lot of impulse spending - maybe on clothing, coffee, or groceries. *Purr*haps you discover that a good chunk of your discretionary spending is on "regrettable" purchases.

Of course, the budget is an important part of helping you plan for your spending to avoid this, but in some ways, it can actually make you more aware of regrettable spending. It can bring up some painful realizations as you track your expenses. Like "Holy kittens I spend a thousand dollars a year on catnip!" (Or whatever your particular affliction is.)

As you start budgeting, you might notice a link between your emotions and your spending. Part of untangling your relationship with money is understanding when your purchasing is driven by emotions. There's a reason that commercials for insurance have tear-jerker tales of kids being reunited with their long-lost parents - manipulating human emotions is an excellent way to drive spending decisions.

Here are some cues you might say when you're justifying emotional spending:

> "I'll feel better if I buy it."
>
> "I can't help it!"
>
> "I deserve it."
>
> "Everyone else has one."
>
> "I just couldn't say no."
>
> "I'll feel more secure."

EMOTIONAL SPENDING TRIGGERS

FEAR

IMPATIENCE

LUST

PAIN

GRIEF

JOY

COMPETITION

Now it's okay to have emotional spending - we all will spend emotionally sometimes. But maybe you realize that when you're feeling sad, you stop by a store on the way home and buy a new outfit or some candy. And later you don't even like those things.

My emotional spending regret has always been stationery supplies when I'm stressed at the office.

I cannot get enough of pretty paper and nice pens - and sometimes, as though brought there through no decision of my own, I find myself browsing the office supply store after a hard day at work.

Studies[5] show when individuals are stressed and feel anxiety, fear, or shame, they feel off-balance and the human brain will attempt to repair or rebalance itself by seeking out impulsive behaviors.

(For example, while stuck on writing this chapter, I decided to go on a used clothing website just to "check in on" some cat print dresses. Because that immediate "ping" of finding something helps offset the hard slog of writing.)

One key element to budgeting is to recognize and plan for feeling some emotions, and then address that in the creation of the budget. That is why it's so important that you build the budget when you're feeling calm and collected, so that the budget can guide you when you are feeling less *calm and collected*. It's a sort of insurance against the fact that you're human, and that being human is hard sometimes.

So, once you start tracking your expenses, you've only tackled one half of the equation - you have the information on your spending but how do you actually stop yourself from running at full-speed across the room like my cat after she's used the litterbox?

Waiting Period

One tactic you can implement to cut down on regrettable emotional spending is a waiting period for all non-necessary purchases. Delayed gratification is not only a good money skill, it's also a good life skill (please feel free to tell my cat that she's gaining moral character by waiting until after 4:30AM to get breakfast).

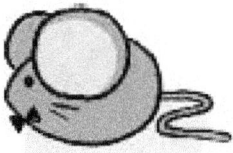

It turns out that waiting 24 or 72 hours or even a few weeks before you hit "buy" on that online cart with a cat snuggie and a mocha-inspired cookbook will often make you realize that was pretty silly, and you definitely wanted those things because you were feeling emotional after watching videos of baby squirrels.

Now, you're saying "But there is only a sale today on that thing! I need it *right meow*!" In some ways, implementing a waiting period can make it easier to spend money quickly when there is a sale and not regret it, because you know it's *actually a good deal* and you're also confident it's something you've wanted for quite awhile. Writing down the item you want can actually help make the purchase feel more "real." Sometimes when I want a non-essential item, I budget for that thing in the next month - because if it turns out that I "left" the money in the category next month instead of moving it around into another category, maybe *I really do* want it.

It's also helpful to link purchases to values and emotions - if you are tracking items you want, feel free to write down the value it represents for you. For items that aren't really "value" focused items, it can help to link the purchase to a values-based goal as a reward. In the case of a nice workout shirt I wanted, I linked it to a fitness-related goal. This means not only do I have a waiting period, I'm going to feel stoked about that shirt every time I wear it because it represents ticking off a big fitness goal for myself. You can even link your purchases to savings goals - for example, if you save $1,000 in your mini emergency fund, you budget to spend $50 on a new video game.

When Regrettable Spending is Essential

One of the hardest parts of budgeting in the beginning for many folks is dealing with essential spending - like food - that is prone to emotional spending. Eating out, especially fast food and bars, can be a regrettable purchase for many.

The goal is to try to get the joy of eating out:

- *Yay! Someone made me food I can't make myself!*
- *Yay! I ate a thing when I was in a rush and it was delicious!*

- *Yay! I had a lovely time with my family and didn't do any dishes!*

Without the regret:

- *Ugh! Why did I spend money on a bad sandwich?*

Try planning for eating out a week or so in advance. This can work even for lunches out at work or coffee - look at your schedule once a week and think, "I am going to see my friend for lunch on Friday, and we're going to go get falafel so I'm marking it in my calendar." The wait and anticipation of eating out is half the fun.

If the social pressure of spending money on lunch at work is getting to you, creating a "packed lunch days" game can really help this behavior. You can track the number of days each week that you pack your lunch, and then reward yourself with a lunch out after a certain number of days. If you plan for that day and get excitement up among yourself (and maybe even your co-workers) for "Falafel Friday," you might find that falafel tastes *that much better* (and is more than offset by the hundreds of dollars a month you save by packing your lunch most days.)

If you have trouble with impulse purchases at the grocery store or mega-market, try shopping with a list and shopping when you are not hungry or thirsty. Thirst actually creates a "stress response" in your body[5] and triggers feelings of scarcity, leaving you with a bunch of candy bars and cute notepads in addition to the gloves you walked in to buy.

You can also try pre-ordering your food for pick up a few days in advance. Behavioral economics research shows we make better decisions about healthy and economical choices in food when we purchase for our future self, and are less likely to see the excellent deal on candy or fancy cheese and buy it at the last moment.

Squashing the Emotional Purchase Bug

If you have an impulse purchase that is part of a predictable pattern, you can try to squash that particular emotional purchase. For example, if you always buy a burrito when you're going home from the therapist because you're feeling Feelings and want to smother them with salsa, consider a few things:

- **Can you change your routine to avoid this?**
- **Is there something free or cheap that you can do to take care of these emotions in a different way?**
- **Is this purchase a thing you actually do want or need?**

In the case of the therapy-salsa loop, you could take a different route home from the therapist that does not go past the burrito restaurant. Or you could change the weekly time slot of your therapy appointment so it coincides less with burrito-craving time of day. Or you perhaps you can get a $2 coffee instead of a $9 burrito. Maybe you can go for a run or long walk to deal with your emotions post-therapy instead.

But consider that processing your therapy feelings with burritos is a Cost Of Being a Human. If you're not going into debt for those couple of burritos each month, maybe you just need to budget for it because it actually is *a value in disguise* (health and stability, *purr*haps?) Maybe you don't want to believe you're the person who smothers raw emotion with black beans, but at this point in your life, you are, and that is **okay.**

This is where the budget comes in: you can use tracking your expenses to recognize patterns, and to accept that you are a human and budget for a little bit of emotional spending. It happens to all of us. Plan for it!

The Budget Check-in

Now you've realized your budget is a custom-made document just for you and have started to build one based on your own goals and values. You've predicted your known unknowns. You're saving some money for yourself. Hopefully you've found a method for tracking your spending. Now here's the magic - you have to actually compare what you spent to the budget!

On a regular basis (weekly is best at first), you're going to create a little ritual where you compare your budget to what you actually spent. You should make this nice for yourself, especially if you're generally anxious about this stuff. Make it a clear-headed time for yourself - with a nice calming beverage at your side. Make sure any kids or kitties are not underfoot and turn off the news in the background. If you do it weekly, it should take less than 30 minutes, or the length of one sitcom episode.

It doesn't matter if this check-in is on paper or on the computer - do whatever you'll stick to. This is where the regular practice part of budgeting comes into play - the check-in gives you the opportunity to see where you're at and make adjustments. It lets you look ahead and make sure there's nothing unexpected coming up soon. The good news is that the more often you do this, the easier it is. Once you get used to this, checking your finances will no longer make you panicked but instead give you a sense of calm, confident control.

Create a relaxing budgeting ritual with tea, candles, kitty snuggles - whatever you need to make your finances less scary.

"I know you really want a new catnip mouse, but we really need to prioritize a new paper bag; the current one is almost completely shredded."

Bringing on Your Pawtner

All this talk about values and goals and emotional spending sounds super-pawsome, but what if your partner, spouse, or co-parent doesn't share your interest in getting your money together?

Obviously, the best case scenario is that your partner wants to get a handle on your finances together, in which case, they can complete all these exercises along with you and participate in the weekly budget check-in. The exercises can provide an opportunity to talk about your long-term goals together. Do you want to buy a house? Fund private school? Travel the world? Start a craft brewery together?

That best case scenario doesn't always happen. If your partner is resistant to making a change - either because they don't think there's a problem or they don't want to put in the work - you can lead by example at first, and leave them out of the exercises. They're dealing with *money scripts* just like you are, and their money script might be telling them that they're always going to be broke, that they're bad at math, or they don't need to worry about money because someday they'll win the lottery.

If They Say: "The Finances are Your Thing, Do Whatever You Want":

Ask them simply to show up to the budget check-in. Once you get them there, ask them about their goals and dreams (not the numbers) and shut up and listen while they answer. Ask them to change at least one budget category, so they feel they've participated.

If They're Overspending and Blowing the Budget: Remind them of your shared goals and ask for possible solutions to the overspending - let them come up with some suggestions. (Options: a cash-only budget for "fun money," giving you a call before they buy something, implementing a waiting period.) Leading with shame or judgement almost never works.

If They Feel Like They're Losing Control: This is an excellent implementation of the "no judgement fun money" category. Each of you gets a budget category you can use in any way you like, without any comments from the other.

If You Don't Share Most Expenses: Talk about your goals and values in the context of your categories that you do share. For example, if you co-parent with someone you don't live with, talk about the kind of schooling or childcare you *both* want for your kids, and leave out judgements on any other budget category. If you share housing but not bank accounts, talk about internet speed and groceries- not their student loans.

Week Two Action Items

Fill in your Kitten Budget

Follow the instructions on page 48 and complete the "Kitten Budget" on page 50. Remember, it won't be *purr*fect the first time, and that's okay! In later chapters, we'll make the budget more comprehensive and talk about computer-based options, but this is meant to get you started *fast*.

Find your accountability paw-tner

This whole thing goes easier if you have an accountability partner to check in with. If you have one, your significant other is the best candidate for your accountability partner. A close friend, roommate, or someone you find in the Oh My Dollar! online community also be a great sounding board. You'll check in with this person every week to let them know how you're doing.

Make the Time

Most of this money stuff is simply prioritizing. Remember - if you don't make your money a priority, no one else will do it for you. Find 1.5 hours each week you can use to work on your budget and work through these chapters - and schedule it in your calendar now! Commit to making a change in your life, and start with making the time.

Extra Credit: Play a Game

The "paperclip game" in the appendix is an excellent icebreaker to play with your partner or family members to start talking about money priorities and values. It takes about 10 minutes, depending on how decisive you are. You can play it alone, too - just make sure that your kitty doesn't try to steal all the paperclips like mine does.

Discussion Questions

*These discussion questions are great if you are going through **A Cat's Guide to Money** with friends - but they're also worth having the conversation with yourself, your accountability partner, or just writing them out below.*

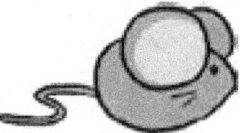

What did you learn by tracking your expenses? Did you find that you fell into "emotional" spending habits often? Were you surprised by what you found?

What category in your budget gives you the most "kitten-like" excitement? Which category fills you with dread?

What do you think your biggest barriers to creating and keeping up a budget will be? Can you create a plan to help overcome those barriers?

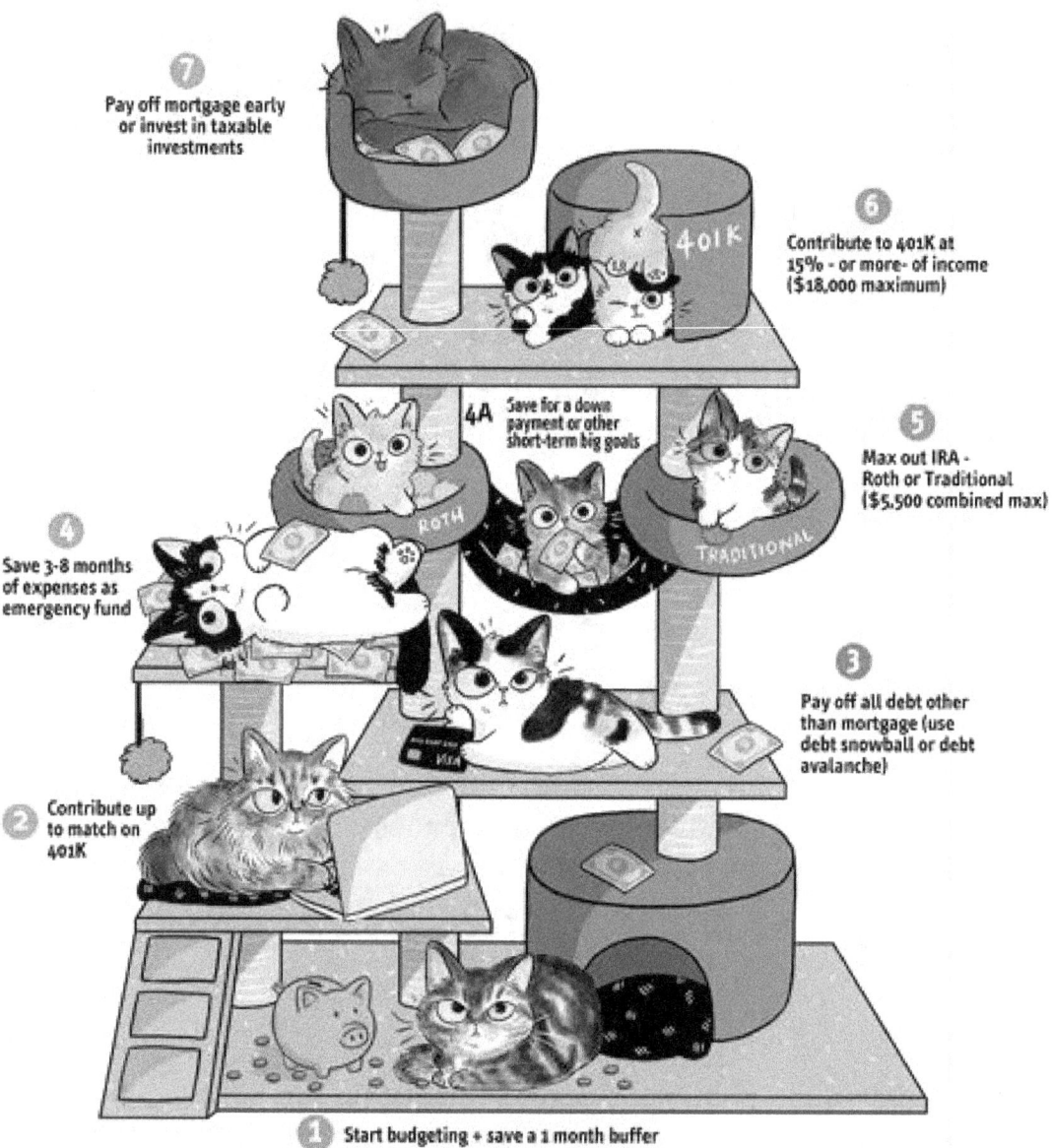

1. Start Budgeting & Save a One Month Buffer (Chapters 2 + 4)

Budgeting is the key to getting a handle on your money, and building up a one month buffer will help handle life's twists.

2. Contribute Up to the Match on 401K (Chapter 5)

If you are offered a match on your retirement savings at work - usually 2-5% - contribute to the match. It's an instant raise, and free money!

3. Pay off All Debt other than Mortgage (Chapter 3)

Debt is the enemy of wealth-building. Focusing on paying on off your debt before you get distracted by other financial goals.

If your total debt is more than 1.5 times your annual income (i.e. your income is $30,000 but you have $50,000 in student loan debt) double your buffer from step 1.

4. Save 3-8 months emergency fund (Chapter 4)

Your emergency fund is your secret weapon. You want to have at least 3 months' expenses available in a liquid account.

4a Save for Down Payment or Other Short-Term goals (Chapter 4)

Save for a down payment for a home or other goals that you'd like to accomplish in the next 3-5 years. Without any debt, you can probably knock out big savings goals faster than you ever thought!

5. Max Out IRA (Chapter 5)

Your IRA - Roth or Traditional - gives you the most flexibility to invest for retirement. Aim to max it out at $6,000 annually (2020 limit).

6. Contribute to 401K at 15% or more of income (Chapter 5)

Your 401K, 403B, or employer pension gives you the advantage of savings pre-tax in a retirement account. If it's possible in your budget, aim to max out the accounts.

7. Pay off mortgage early or invest in other instruments

You've made it to the top! Once you've maxed your retirement, consider paying off your mortgage early, investing in taxable investments or businesses, or giving charitably in your community.

Debt, the Financial Litterbox
Cleaning up the Mess

Debt is one of the best-marketed tools of the past half-decade. MasterCard, Visa, and student loans didn't exist just 65 years ago. But now we're taught that debt is a required part of the American lifestyle.

To get a job, we take out student loans. To get to work, we need a car loan. To get suits to wear to our job, we take out a store card. To get a couch to sit on after work, we buy it now and pay back in installments. To get a house to put the couch in, we take out a mortgage. To pay off the credit cards bills from furnishing the house, we take out an equity loan.

American life has become an endless treadmill of debt options invading places that we never thought they would before - you can even take out a loan for a vacation. Debt has been marketed in so many forms and so aggressively that even *believing* that you can live debt-free requires a mindset shift from normal.

But do you want to be normal? Because normal is pretty broke. Is being "normal" so great if it forces you to be stuck in the financial litterbox?

If you're going to get your money together, one of the key things you can do is understand that debt is the biggest barrier to your financial well-being. To do that you have to build up armor against the messages that society tells you about debt - that everyone has it and that it's perfectly acceptable.

There's a reason that debt has been sold as a part of modern life. Debt is profitable for big companies and banks. Many large clothing retailers make more profit on credit card financing than they do on clothing. Corporations have learned that if they sell you the image of success as having shiny things, they can make twice as much money by also selling you the debt financing to acquire that shiny thing *before* you can afford it. Not only that, they can raise Shiny Thing's price higher and higher, because now instead of looking at the full price, you're only looking at the monthly payment.

**Chris
Los Angeles, CA
PopcornFinance.com**

Marketers offer debt as a "relaxing" alternative to saving for a purchase or doing without. One of the major providers of "buy now, pay later" furniture loans - also sold as "rent to own" (which are marketed primarily to the working class) uses the tagline ***Relaxation Made Easy.*** It's profitable to distract consumers with 0% down on a couch - take it home now, relax, pay nothing - and fail to mention that after interest, they'll pay $2,000 for that $800 couch. There's nothing wrong with a nicely furnished home, but it's the most profitable to convince consumers that *they deserve it right meow.*

But if the same consumers had to cut back on current expenses to save up for a $2,000 couch in cash, they might decide to get a cheaper couch or do without. Debt provides a way they can get it right now - and their Future Self can worry about saving to pay for it.

Debt, in its many forms, is the enemy of wealth-building. You don't have to aspire to be filthy rich to see that paying on debt is exhausting - someone else is making money off your money, and you have to pay it back under their terms. ***You will change your life*** if you embrace the idea that paying for things in full when you purchase them is more powerful than being in debt to someone else.

If you're trapped in the typical modern consumer mindset, you're going to need a mindset shift to embrace that idea. Escaping the treadmill of debt requires you to get completely fed up with being in the financial litterbox. It requires you to truly believe that being "only a little behind" isn't acceptable.

Getting out of the financial litterbox, most of all, requires you to stop comparing your life to others - and start focusing on your own sense of calm around your money. You'll have to get out of the habit of saying "I can afford this" when you mean that you can afford the monthly payment on borrowing money.

You have to say "I can afford this" only when you can pay for it all, in cash, right now while still meeting your other goals and financial obligations.

I also want to emphasize that **having debt does not make you a bad person.** Your choices with money in the past have nothing to do with your integrity and worth as a person. **You are worthy no matter your financial situation**. The last thing I want you to feel at the end of this chapter is shame. I want you to be mad at the debt itself, not angry at yourself for getting into debt. Past You can't feel it when you get angry at them.

There's societal reasons that many of us have taken on debt: the broken American health care system leaves many of us climbing up a mountain of medical debt. And once federal student loans became available in the late 1950's, the sticker price of higher education climbed at levels never seen

before (8 times the rate of inflation.)[6] Many of us took out loans at overpriced and underfunded colleges in order to have a stable and secure job. This perpetuated a cycle where higher education, instead of being seen as a way to broaden the mind, became exclusively a job-training program - because students needed to land well-paying jobs post-graduation in order to service their student loan debts.

I understand there's a strong temptation to be angry at the system, to be mad at the societal problems that landed you in debt. But dwelling on that is unlikely to change your own situation (but if you want to work on reforming financial consumer policy, though, we could all use your passion!)

Paying off your debt isn't overly complicated, but it does take persistence and patience. You have to learn to hate the debt that you have and want nothing more than for it to be gone. As you get further into paying off your debt and budgeting, you'll start to realize that just like all other budgetary decisions, *everything you do* is a tradeoff against paying off debt. Cutting your cell phone bill by $25 a month could carve 3 years off your student loan repayment. Taking the bus to work instead of driving for a few months could get you out from under a payday loan in months instead of years.

Looking at debt payoff in the context of the whole budget can help highlight the tradeoffs that you're making. Sometimes what seems like the best path forward initially doesn't necessarily make sense when you consider the ripple effects.

If you take a second job to help pay down debt, but the stress of the second job leads you pick up an extra bottle of wine and some gossip magazines on the way home, and on the odd night you have to pay a babysitter when you're working, you might not actually be paying off your debt faster - you might just be taking a second job to pay for wine, magazines, gas to work, and babysitters. You might be better off putting in overtime or cutting out your gym membership instead. Using the budget to look at your choices in context of your entire life helps show those ripple effects.

I have yet to meet someone who tells me one of their core values in life is "paying interest to large multi-national banks." Paying off your debt is a fantastic way to stick it to the Man and get your money back to spend on ***your own values.***

Kitten Laser Focus

It can be easy to focus only on the monthly payments and ignore the long-term view of debt. But if you want to get rid of your debt, you have to make a plan of attack that looks at the big picture - that means you need to consider the long term costs of your interest payments.

When my kitty wants to jump from the counter to top of the fridge, she looks at the fridge, the floor, and mentally calculates the angles and speed she'll travel at. She takes in the whole view, and then she focuses in exactly where she needs to land.

My cat recently noticed a place where the paint chipped off the wall and she spent days staring at that spot with complete focus, waiting for the "bug" to move. You can apply that same level of focus (with a bit more

strategy) to your debts.

You know how when a kitten sees a laser pointer, they can't focus on anything else? They become completely and utterly entranced by that little red dot and their only ambition in the world is to attack and destroy that dot. That's what you need to be like with your debt.

You must maintain focus on the goal at hand, and not get distracted by fancier cars, houses, or other conflicting goals. The goal is to destroy your debt, just like that little red dot.

Good Debt vs. Bad Debt

You may have heard about "good debt" versus "bad debt". Good debt is sometimes seen as educational debt or debt to purchase a home, while bad debt is car loans, personal loans, or consumer debt. In reality, this is a false accounting method, debt is not good or bad - it is just that, debt. It's simply a negative number in your personal balance sheet, and doesn't come with a morality rating.

There is one definition you should be aware of, however: secured debt versus unsecured debt. Unsecured debt is when there's nothing to take away if you can't repay (education can't be sucked out of your brain, the credit card company can't take back those brunches you ate) whereas secured debt is a car loan or mortgage where the creditor can *repossess* (take away) the item if you fail to pay.

Snowballs and Avalanches

There's two main strategies for paying off debt quickly: debt snowball and debt avalanche. The debt snowball method is based in behavioral science, while the debt avalanche method is more mathematically sound. It doesn't really matter which method you choose, you just need to choose a strategy and go for it. One of the biggest mistakes that people make with debt payoff is to get overwhelmed by their debts and doing nothing (or choosing a strategy of "random panic".)

The first thing you need to for either method is write down all your debts -

record the minimum monthly payments, the interest rate, and the total owed. Don't include your first mortgage for this exercise, but include any second mortgage or home equity lines of credit. You can use the debt worksheet on the next page to list them all out, or you can head over to undebt.it and use the debt calculator. If you aren't sure what all your debts are, you can check out annualcreditreport.com to look up your creditors, and National Student Loan Data System (nslds.ed.gov) to look up all your student loans.

Debt Snowball

The debt snowball is the behavioral method of debt payoff. The snowball method focuses on *changing behavior*. The debt snowball is best at two things: giving you earlier "wins" in your debt payoff to keep you motivated, and helping reduce the total amount of payments you need to juggle. It's a great method if you don't have a lot of discretionary income after debt service.

For the debt snowball, you will pay all your minimum payments on your debt, putting any extra money into paying off the smallest total debt first (no matter what the interest rate is).

Once that smallest debt is totally paid off, you will take the minimum payment from that debt, plus your extra payment, and apply it to the next smallest debt. It gathers up extra money just like rolling a snowball in a pile of snow, and as you go down your list of debts, your "snowball" will get bigger and bigger.

The debt snowball rolls your extra payments up. (I cannot guarantee your snowball will be this cute.)

On the reverse page is a sample worksheet for Mittens, who is paying off her debt using the debt snowball method - paying as much extra as she can on the lowest balance debt (the hospital bill), regardless of interest rate.

As you pay off your smallest debt, your "snowball" - the amount you can pay towards your remaining debt - will get bigger and bigger.

She can pay $300 extra each month on top of her minimum payments. When she has finished off her hospital bill in 3 month's time, she'll then apply the $320 ($20 minimum payment + $300 extra) towards her visa card, which has the second lowest balance at $3,000.

If she sticks with this plan, she'll pay off all her debt in 45 months and pay $3,767 in interest.

Debt	Total Amount	Interest Rate	Minimum Payment (I)	Extra	Total Payment (I + II)
HOSPITAL BILL	$1000	0%	$20	$300	$320
VISA CARD	$3,000	20.2%	$50	$0	$50
FEDERAL STUDENT LOAN	$5,500	6.8%	$63	$0	$63
PRIVATE STUDENT LOAN	$12,000	8.9%	$151	$0	$151
Total					$584

Debt Avalanche

The debt avalanche is a method where you pay all your minimum payments on your debt, and put any extra debt payoff money into paying off the highest interest rate debt first. Once that debt is paid off, you then put any "extra" money into the next highest interest rate, and so forth.

Each time you pay off a debt, your overall monthly budget for debt payoff stays the same, but the amount you can apply to your target debt grows larger. This means your debt payoff gets faster and more powerful - and increases the speed at which your debt goes away forever.

The debt avalanche is technically the most mathematically efficient way to pay off debt (you'll pay less interest overall and it will be the fastest debt payoff) but if your highest interest debt is the biggest total balance, it can be discouraging. If you have a lot of little debts to keep track of - like small 0% interest medical debts, it can leave you with a lot of extra payments for longer.

If Mittens decided to use the debt avalanche method for the same debts she had on page 75, she'd instead list her debts from highest to lowest interest rate, and would apply her extra $300 payment towards her Visa card first. Avalanche method has her paying lower interest overall ($3,281) but only speeds up the repayment timeline by 1 month.

Debt (list name and type)	Total Amount	Interest Rate	Minimum Payment (I)	Extra Payment (II)	Total
VISA CARD	$3,000	20.2%	$50	$300	$350
PRIVATE STUDENT LOAN	$12,000	8.9%	$151	$0	$151
FEDERAL STUDENT LOAN	$5,500	6.8%	$63	$0	$63
HOSPITAL BILL	$1000	0%	$20	$0	$20
Total					$584

The Bottom Line

It's not important which method you choose - they both have advantages. The most important is to pick a method, and stick with it. Instead of acting randomly and throwing extra dollar bills into envelopes and mailing them off to creditors hoping it helps, following a thought-out debt payoff plan (any one you like) is what will help you actually get out of debt.

Depending on the types and mixes of interest rates for your debt (or the forgiveness policy on your student loans) different payoff strategies might make a big difference in your repayment timeline until you are debt-free. It's worth taking the hour to input your loans into a debt payoff calculator, such as the one at **undebt.it** to figure out which method would work the best for your budget and your situation.

The Simple Steps Of Paying off Debt

Remember: you cannot get out of debt effectively if you keep getting yourself into more debt. Set aside your one-month buffer and establish sinking funds to help prevent you from taking out more debt - and put down the credit cards.

1. Create a list of all your debts. This might require you to dig up some logins to your student loans and credit cards, track down some mail from the doctor. Set aside the time to find everything you need to find all your debts. Write down the name, the total balance owed, your minimum payments, and find the interest rate.

2. Put your debts in order - for debt avalanche, put them in order from highest interest rate to lowest interest rate. For debt snowball, put them in order by smallest balance to largest balance. Remember, the most important thing about picking a strategy is that you pick one. Choose at random if you have to! Don't get stressed out over choosing the strategy. Inaction is worse for your finances than the few dollars of difference between the strategies.

3. Pay your minimum payments on every single debt (every time, all the time) – except the first one. Put every extra dollar you can find towards paying off that first debt. Pick up overtime or another side gig, sell your belongings, negotiate your internet bill, do what you need to do to get some extra cash. (Do *not* start a business that requires you to take out more debt to earn extra money, though).

4. Budget a small treat for yourself in order to recognize the accomplishment and keep your motivation going! *Throw yourself a party when you pay off that first debt. Just a little (frugal) party - but a party nonetheless (a good book in the bathtub anyone?)*

5. Take the amount you were paying towards the first debt and put towards the next debt on the list. Do this until this one is paid off. Keep paying your minimum payments on all your debts (every time,

all the time). ***Another frugal party to celebrate the accomplishment!!***

6. Continue this process until each one is paid off. Simple, but not easy. But I know you're up for it.

The Minimum Payment Trap

Buying things on credit costs more. It's that simple. You pay interest for the privilege of getting the thing ***right meow*** and then repaying it later.

If you look on your credit card statement (if you get online statements, you'll have to download the PDF) you will see that there is a paragraph that tells you how long it will take you to pay off total balance if you pay only the minimum payment.

If your APR (Annual Percentage Rate - the interest rate you pay per year) is 18-25%, a typical credit card interest rate, you could end up paying ten times more on your initial purchase by only paying the minimum payment.

Making only the minimum payment on credit cards is a trap many kittens fall into when they get credit cards - not realizing just how expensive that is over the long term.

ITEM	ORIGINAL PRICE	APR	INTEREST PAID	TOTAL PAID	YEARS TO PAY OFF
Game System	$500	18%	$439	$939	8
Laptop	$2,500	18%	$2,899	$8,781	34
Cat Castle	$1,000	18%	$1,899	$2,899	18

Many people don't realize that 0% down, 12-month-repayment programs for purchases like laptops are actually branded credit cards that convert to 20-30% APR credit cards at the end of the 12 months. This is why it's important to read the fine print!

Getting around like a smart kitten

Cars are one of the things that modern society conditions you to believe must be financed. How else can you get to work other than a $22,000 car on low monthly payments?

Advertisers prey on your emotions - telling you need a new car to be safer for your family or look cool to other Tom Cats. Why? Because it's profitable to get you to finance a car and they know it's unlikely the average American has $22,000 in cash just sitting around. Car dealerships make more of their profit off of financing than they do off the cars themselves.

Paying for a used car in cash is the smartest option for all kittens. If it's not a possibility for you, you want to aim for the lowest interest rate possible, and get the interest rate baked into your monthly payments (called an "installment loan") rather than an loan with compounding interest. Ideally, your monthly car costs, including car payment, maintenance, insurance and gas, should be no more than 10% of your take-home pay (remember to consider the rest of your budget in context, your mileage may vary.) Transportation is one of the "big three" (housing, transportation, and food) costs that drastically influence your overall budget, and if you can reduce your expense, you'll see a much bigger win than cutting coupons.

If your total vehicle value (cars, motorcycles, etc) is more than half your annual income, you are considered "car poor". This means owning $20,000 car on a $30,000 income would put you in the "car poor" category. Because most cars lose value every year, ideally you don't want too much of your wealth tied up in things that roll around. Of course, it's your choice based on your own values and needs (some folks that need adaptive vehicles might be "car poor" with few other transportation options).

The coolest cats drive paid off Catillacs.

There are many car lots that prey on the low income or folks with low or no credit scores, called "Buy Here Pay Here". If you're unable to get a regular car loan, these sketchy places are happy to help you find a way to finance a car at exorbitant interest rates. Their business models bet on most customers not being able to repay the loan, and they have extremely high default and repossession rates.[7]

If you're living paycheck to paycheck, you're better off saving in cash for a cheaper car or approaching your credit union or bank for a lower interest loan. "Buy Here Pay Here" lots are about as scary to your wealth as the vacuum cleaner is to my cat.

Leasing a Car is like renting the litterbox and Paying extra for the Turds

Leasing a car is rarely a good option - it's the worst of financing combined with the worst of renting, in many ways - you pay a high monthly fee, but can recoup none of the costs at the end of your lease by selling the car, plus often they tack on fees for "wear and tear". They even charge you for going over the specified allotment of miles - and that can cost thousands of dollars.

Buying a car is almost always cheaper in the long run. If you aren't able to afford the monthly payment on a car except if you are to lease it, then you can't afford that model of car and should choose a lower-end model or a used car - quite simply, leasing is not a way to build wealth, and except in extremely rare circumstances, is a way to sell you something you can't afford (that you don't get to keep.)

Other options

If you're working on paying off debt or want to save up money to buy a car in cash, investigate other transportation options. You can always try out:

- Public transportation
- Carpooling with coworkers
- Riding a bicycle or skateboard to work (can be excellent for your health, too)
- Working from home one or more days a week to cut down your commute
- Getting a car-sharing membership, like Zipcar or Car2Go

- Using ride-hailing apps like Uber or Lyft when you're in a pinch
- The old classic: walking!

Purrfecting Your Loan Payoff

Navigating student loans in the United States can sometimes feel like you need a PHD in student loan repayment all by itself. One of the most important things to understand is that student loans are the stickiest kinds of debt - even bankruptcy won't get rid of student debt. So having a payoff plan for your student loans is essential to your long term financial well-being.

When you're crafting your student loan repayment, the first thing to get a handle on is what and who you owe. For this step, you need to figure out who your loan providers are. The way loans work in the US is that quite often your total loan is split up between multiple providers.

Katie
Chicago, IL

For your federal loans (meaning non-private ones) the best place to go is the NSLDS (National Student Loan Data System). You'll need to know your FSA ID (the thing you logged into the FAFSA with). This is important because you will use it to access the various government websites that show you your federal loans. If you don't remember it or can't find it, you can reset it at *https://studentaid.ed.gov* - or you can call the federal student aid department and they'll walk you through it.

The NSLDS does not have data on older loans — for example, ones borrowed in the 1980s. It also doesn't list medical and nursing school loans or private loans. If you have loans that are in one of those categories that are still in repayment, you'll have to locate them by looking at your credit report.

You can get a free credit report from the three main credit reporting agencies — Experian, TransUnion, and Equifax — by visiting *annualcreditreport.com*. These will list all the loans out under your name. You can also use a free credit reporting website like creditkarma.com or creditsesame.com to look at a prettier version of your report. I recommend ordering your credit report but also using one of the easier-to understand websites to get a cleaner looking overview.

The goal is to go on a fact-finding mission. The best way to approach this is like a detective. Cool and detached - try to take shame out of the equation (I know that's easier said than done). It's possible you may have to make a lot of soul-sucking calls.

If you have trouble figuring out who you owe, you can call up the bursar's office at your alma mater and ask for your records. You may get forwarded to financial aid or you may find out you've been sent to collections, in which case, please find out the number of the agency. Just try to find out that number. If you owe a balance to your college, keep asking about payment plans. If you owe, for example $2,000, ask them if you can pay it over 12 months. Keep asking for a payment plan and don't stop until you get something you can afford.

Once you have a list of all your loans (list them out on the debt repayment worksheet), you can login into **studentloans.gov** and use the repayment plan estimator to see what different repayment options you have. You can do this even for loans that are private. You need to figure out what is affordable to you. If you have variable income, you want to choose a repayment amount that is affordable on your lowest-earning months (you can always pay back more than the minimum).

Federal Repayment Plan Types

Standard Plan

This plan is cheapest over time but the highest monthly payment. The standard repayment term is 10 years.

Graduated

Your student loan payments will increase over time, starting out lower than the standard repayment, but increasing every 2 years up to 10 years (not including deferment or forbearance). This is not the same as income based repayment plans. The downside of this plan is that you have no guarantee your income will go up every two years.

Extended Repayment Plan

If you have taken out more than $30,000 of qualifying federal loans, you can extend your repayment timeline from 10 years out to 25 years. You will pay more interest under this plan, but your monthly payment will be lower.

Income Based Repayment (IBR)

If you are low income and having trouble meeting your minimum payments, this type of repayment plan is usually the best option, where your payment is set at 10-15% of your discretionary income. You can enroll in income-driven repayment plans even if you are unemployed and making $0. With a $0 monthly income, your payments would be $0 but you would still be in good standing on your loans (though they would keep accruing interest). If you haven't paid off your loan in 20 or 25 years, the balance will be forgiven (but the amount forgiven may be taxed).

Pay As You Earn Repayment Plan (PAYE/REPAYE)

This plan will set your payment based on your income, and will be no more than 10% of your discretionary income. If your loans were taken out before July 2014, you may pay less on PAYE than on IBR. If you haven't paid off your loan in 20 years, the balance will be forgiven (but the amount forgiven may be taxed).

Joe and Ali, now continual world travelers

Income Contigent Repayment (ICR)

Similar to IBR and PAYE/REPAYE, this repayment plan is based off your discretionary income, but it will set your payment amount at 20 percent of your discretionary income or the amount a standard loan would get repaid after 12 years.

Forgiveness, Discharge, and Cancellation

There are very few ways to get your student loans to "disappear" other than to pay them off. But here are a few programs you should know about.

Public Service Loan Forgiveness

This forgiveness program is for folks working in paid, full-time (at least 30 hours/week) positions at qualifying public service organizations (government organizations, rural health care, or 501(c)3 nonprofits.) Every year you must send in a federal form certifying your employment. You must be in a qualifying public service role for 10 years (though you can change employers) and you must make 120 on-time monthly payments on your loans. You must be on a income-driven repayment plan to utilize this forgiveness. This program is under political debate, and may not continue to exist.

Teacher Loan Forgiveness Program & Perkins Cancellation

For teaching professionals working full-time in certain types of schools (low-income, high-demand, or special education), you can be eligible for forgiveness of your direct subsidized student loans under the Teacher Loan Forgiveness Program after 5 years. Under the same qualifications, Perkins loans will be canceled a percentage each year spent working in a school, up to 100 percent after 5 years.

Forbearance and Deferment

Deferment is a temporary suspension of loan payments for specific situations, such as returning to higher education or short-term emergencies. Forbearance is a temporary reduction of payments. You may end up accruing additional interest on the loan, making your loans cost more overall. If your short-term emergency is unemployment or some other loss of income, it's better to switch to an income-driven repayment plan where your payment may drop to $0.

Disability Discharge

If you are permanently disabled, you can get most federal loans discharged. You do not have to be receiving SSDI or SSI in order to be considered disabled, but you do need a doctor's statement of disability.

Delinquency

Being delinquent on your student loans is when you have not made a payment for 90 days. The fastest way out of being delinquent is to make a payment.

Recovering from Default

Your loans are considered in default if you do not make payments over a period of 270 days. You *can* recover from defaulting on student loans, especially early in the process. So if you get one of those scary letters in the mail, don't completely panic.

You can eliminate the loan default by "rehabilitating" a defaulted loan. You will have to call your loan provider - possibly a collections agency, depending on how defaulted you are, in order to get your loan in rehabilitation. To qualify for loan rehabilitation for most loans, you have to make nine monthly payments within 20 days of the due date during a period of 10 consecutive months. The 9 out of 10 rule basically allows you to miss your payment one month, but still be eligible to rehabilitate. For the Perkins loans you have to make 9 out of 9 payments on time.

One thing that's important to both prevent defaulting again AND save you money - Some lenders offer a 0.25% discount on your interest rate if you sign up for automatic payments! So do it!

Teacher Loan Forgiveness Program & Perkins Cancellation

For teaching professionals working full-time in certain types of schools (low-income, high-demand, or special education), you can be eligible for forgiveness of your direct subsidized student loans under the Teacher Loan Forgiveness Program after 5 years. Under the same qualifications, Perkins loans will be canceled a percentage each year spent working in a school, up to 100 percent after 5 years.

Forbearance and Deferment

Deferment is a temporary suspension of loan payments for specific situations, such as returning to higher education or short-term emergencies. Forbearance is a temporary reduction of payments. You may end up accruing additional inte on the loan, making your loans cost more overall. If your short-term emergency is unemployment or some other loss of income, it's better to switch to an income-driven repayment plan where your payment may drop to $0.

That was the last time we left Maximus with matches and piles of student loan mail.

Private Student Loans

Private loans are unfortunately some of the most frustrating loans out there, because they often have much higher interest rates than federal loans and have some of the least flexible repayment plans. In the case of your private student loans, you must work out a repayment plan with your lender. If you are low-income, you'll get the most payment flexibility from an income-driven repayment plan for federal loans, allowing you to budget more to get rid of the private student loans!

Private loan consolidation/refinancing

If you have a high interest rate - over 7% - for your private loans, you can look into refinancing or consolidating (combining) your private loans. There are a number of student loan refinancers out there, but you usually need a good credit score and decent income to qualify for a lower monthly payment. If you are considering refinancing, shop around and get the companies to compete for your business, aiming for the lowest interest rate. You almost never want to refinance federal loans!

Spotting a student loan scam

Student loan "relief" companies like to prey on the scared. They use official-sounding names like "Federal" or "National", and they'll offer immediate relief from your loan payments. Consolidation and refinancing is something you can do on your own, for no extra fee, and no private company can "make your loans disappear!" Run, far away if any "student loan relief" company demands up-front payment!

AN EXTRA $75 PER MONTH CAN SAVE YOU 7 YEARS

Just a small amount extra can make a huge difference in the length of your student loan. If you can find an extra $75 dollars each month to put towards your loan, you could be debt-free 7 years earlier and save $7,000 like the below example.

Bigger amounts have an outsized effect thanks to compound interest - doubling your payment on the below loan gets you free in 6 years!

PAYING $175 PER MONTH – 17.6 YEARS
$22,000 STUDENT LOAN AT 6.8% INTEREST
$37,009 TOTAL PAID / $15,009 PAID IN INTEREST

PAYING $250 PER MONTH – 10 YEARS
$22,000 STUDENT LOAN AT 6.8% INTEREST
$29,967 TOTAL PAID / $7,967 PAID IN INTEREST

Consolidation

Consolidation - combining your payments - often seems like a magic solution, but usually changing your repayment plan to an income-driven repayment plan will lower your payment more than consolidation will. What consolidation *can do* is simplify your life. Instead of three different laser pointer dots to chase, you'll only have one.

Consolidation combines your loans into one loan and your new loan will take on the average interest rate. If you choose to consolidate your federal loans you should do so BEFORE you make qualifying payments because your consolidated loan is considered a new loan and you'll be starting from square one with programs like Public Service Loan Forgiveness. (You never want to consolidate Perkins loans due to some special programs that only Perkins loans qualify for.)

Filing a complaint

If a loan servicer is not being helpful, is withholding information about your loans, or is not letting you switch payment plans, you can file a complain with a student loan ombudsman (find the contact information at studentaid.ed.gov).

Week Three Action Items

Make a list of your debts

Are you ready to commit to knocking your debt out? Awesome! It's time to craft your strategy. Complete the debt payoff worksheet on the next page or use one of the online resources mentioned in this chapter to make a list of your debts. Figure out using debt snowball or debt avalanche how long it would take you to be totally free of your non-mortgage debt.

Check in Your Kitten Budget

Have you completely abandoned your kitten budget or have you been faithfully sticking to it? Or are you somewhere in between? Figure out what is and isn't working for you on your budget. If nothing about your initial budget is working for you, revisit the different budgeting strategies on page 47 and try to find a new method that works for you.

Debt Payoff Worksheet

Once you've finished saving your one month buffer, it's time to focus on getting rid of your debt. It can be scary to list all your debts in one place, but acknowledging them is the first step to paying them off. The key to accelerating your debt pay off is that once you've paid off your first debt, apply the minimum payment to the next debt as an extra payment. You'll gain momentum as you go along the way, like rolling a snowball. Refer back to pages 74 and 76 for examples.

Debt	Total Amount	Interest Rate	Minimum Payment (I)	Extra Payment (II)	Total Payment (I + II)

Discussion Questions

These discussion questions are great if you are going through Get Your Money Together with friends - but they're also worth having the conversation with yourself, your accountability partner, or just writing them out below.

Consumer debt was not commonplace just 60 years ago, but now we're taught it is an unavoidable part of American life. Talk about what you've been taught about debt - and how having debt makes you feel.

Often, people's shame about talking about debt means that they are compelled to hide it and not deal with it at all. Why do you think having conversations about money is an important part of dealing with your debt?

What would your life look like right now if you were totally free of debt? What would you be able to do?

Bury that Treasure
Learning to love saving

My cat Dora likes to pick up her sparkly ball and carry it confidently over to her food dish, and then gently place it inside. She'll then leave the ball there for several days, eating around it, before taking it back out to soccer dribble it across the apartment (where it will ultimately end up under the fridge for me to dig out).

Maybe she's "seasoning" the toy for later, or purrhaps she just wants to store her toys in a safe, predictable place. Whatever her reasoning, her strategy of anticipating future needs and taking a long pause between acquiring a sparkly ball and giving it away (to the fridge gap) is exactly the same strategy you can take with your money.

The longer you go between acquiring money and spending it, the more likely you are to be financially well. If you immediately have to spend every penny you make on expenses, it's really hard to get ahead. Increasing the time between earning a dollar and spending it is one part of helping you change your financial stress levels.

I know savings sounds really boring and obvious, but it's my favorite part of financial planning. Savings is doing something for yourself - it's *paying yourself!* It's also, unfortunately, pretty uncommon in our culture.

Savings is a key part of taking control of your money. But of course, savings takes diligence and time, and other things will always try to get in the way - debt payments, vacations, sick days, car repairs. If you want to get ahead with your money, you have to make saving money a clear *purr*iority for yourself and pay yourself before you pay everyone else. If you don't save for yourself, mostly likely, no one else will do it for you.

Saving up your one Month Buffer

On the cat tree of financial priorities (page 56), the very first goal is to start budgeting and build up a one month buffer. A one month buffer is a month's expenses (not necessarily income) that lives inside your checking account or the account you pay bills out of. This savings is not meant to be your emergency fund - or your fun money. The one month buffer acts as a protective layer between your regular spending and your bank account hitting $0. It will help lengthen the amount of time between acquiring money and spending it - which as Dora has shown us, is an excellent way to start building good financial habits (or handle your sparkly balls).

The reason that a one month buffer is your first savings priority is because a month is the most common recurring expense interval. Most folks pay their housing, debt payments, and utilities on a monthly basis. If you have you have a one month buffer in place, you will be able to set many of these expenses on auto payment, simplifying your life and helping your credit by reducing the risk of forgetting a payment (or not having enough left over after groceries to pay your light bill).

The one month buffer comes before aggressively paying off debt in your goals because if you don't have any savings at all, it's likely you'll take out debt to cover an unexpected expenses.

This one month buffer is also helping buy you flexibility to adapt and change to unexpected circumstances. Thirty days is often enough time to start figuring out a new plan if your current life goes sideways: it's a common notice period to cancel contracts or leases or search for a new place to live.

If you haven't been in the habit of saving, building up a month of savings can feel really daunting, but I promise it is an achievable number. You only need two things to build up savings: living below your income, and time. Time is already inevitable. Time will pass regardless of whether or not you're saving money, so you might as well use it to your advantage!

If you can save $60 out of each paycheck, and you spend $1,560 per month, it will take you a year to build up a one-month savings buffer. That can seem like a long amount of time to some. But if you've been living paycheck-to-paycheck for a long time, imagine a year ago you had started saving for your buffer and you had a one-month buffer in place right now.

How would you feel right now? Would you thank your past self for the foresight to make that choice? The next year is going to pass regardless, so you might as well start saving.

One thing you'll notice is that if you start intentionally working towards a savings goal and tracking how you're doing, your progress will almost inevitably get faster than you originally planned. If you are able to sell a few things you no longer need (or realize you can't afford, like a financed car) or can save your tax refund check, you might be able to get that buffer set up in just a few weeks' time.

If you have a lot of debt - more than 150% of your annual income in debt (so if you make $40,000 a year but have $60,000 in student loan debt) - you may want to prioritize a bigger savings goal than just the one-month buffer before aggressively paying down your debt with *kitten laser focus* simply because it might take you longer than a few years to pay off your debt.

Emergency Funds

As you move up levels in the financial cat tree, you'll see that saving up an emergency fund comes right after paying off debt and contributing up to the match on your 401K. Emergency funds are an incredibly important part of building your financial well-being, because they help you prepare for the unexpected.

How much to save in your emergency fund is a pretty individual decision, and it has to do with a number of personal factors. Most people should have at least 3 months' expenses in an emergency fund as protection against loss of income, but up to 8 months' expenses can make sense depending on your source of income and lifestyle.

Here are some considerations you can use to determine your own savings goal:

How Flexible your Expenses are

If your expenses are more flexible, you need less savings because you can adjust your lifestyle to make up for a loss in income or traumatic event. For example, if you have a 30 year mortgage, your housing expenses are much less flexible than a month-to-month lease because it will take longer to sell a house than get out of a lease. Remember that debt payments count as expenses, too. So if most of your debts are federal student loans, they're considered "flexible", as it's easier to adjust those in case of lost income than it is to adjust a car payment.

Your Income Predictability and Stability

If you have unstable income, you want to have more in your emergency fund to make up for the possibility of slow or no income months. More unstable income would be a freelancer, a service industry job in a winter tourist town, or a commission-only salesperson. A more stable source of income would be a salaried tenured job or an guaranteed annuity.

How Long to find a New Job with Your Education and Experience

If you're in a tightly regulated industry in a small town, it may take a long time to find a new job and go through background checks. But if you are in an in-demand field with fast hiring - like a software engineer in Silicon Valley during a boom - you could probably find a job quickly. If you've spent most of your career as a highly specialized worker trained in a specific task, like a nuclear reactor operator, your income is considered hard to replace because you'd have to train in a new field or move if something happened to your position (if, for example, the nuclear reactor closed down).

How big your out-of-pocket maximum is on your health insurance

We'll cover insurance more in Chapter 8, but knowing the out-of-pocket maximum on your health insurance can help you plan for a traumatic event. If your out-of-pocket maximum is, say $6,000, you may want to make that a minimum goal for your emergency fund.

Your emergency fund is your ticket out of bad situations: a bad relationship, a bad roommate, a bad job, a hurricane, a car crash. Having a stash of money cannot solve every problem, but it certainly can make a lot of bad situations a little easier.

Stop being surprised by Cucumbers

The other day I found a cache of videos on Youtube of cats being surprised by cucumbers. (You might have seen these, and if you haven't, take a break and go watch a few.) The cats will be sitting calmly, most often eating food, and a cucumber will be placed behind them. When they turn around and see the cucumber, they jump 2 feet into the air with surprise.

This is what many people are like with big expenses. They leap right out of their skin, believing there was no way they could've expected a cucumber to be sitting behind them. I see this regularly with expenses that are totally predictable - replacing household appliances, paying for a wedding, vacations, or replacing their glasses. If you have a vague idea that an expense is coming up at some point in the future, you can establish a savings plan for it.

Perhaps you know you'll have to travel on short notice to visit an aging loved one. Price out the most expensive last minute ticket or rental car, and start putting aside money in your budget for it every month. Give yourself the grace of a savings plan so you don't have to miss an opportunity to spend time with those that matter most to you.

Wear glasses? What does it cost for you to get the most blinged-out glasses? Last time I got glasses, I didn't shell out for the anti-reflective coating because I was too cheap. Let me serve as a lesson to you: anti-reflective coating is modern optometry magic & totally worth the extra $115.

If you own your own home, you can look around at your household appliances. Do you know the age of your water heater? Most water heaters only last 8-10 years, so if yours is 8 years old, you might want to start planning for its replacement. Before your roof is leaking is the best time to start saving up for a roof replacement.

Have a tent & sleeping bag that are patched within an inch of their life? Figure out what a replacement would cost you and make a plan to replace it before you're in the woods.

This works even with future purchases that are undefined. A few years ago, I really wanted to travel on the trans-siberian railway from Russia to China, a 6-day train journey. I didn't know exactly how much it would cost or when I would have the time to make the trip, but I spent about 30 minutes googling some cost estimates and put money aside towards the trip anytime I had extra. And in 2017, I had enough money to take the trip, paying for it entirely in cash - despite it being one of my lowest earning years.

The most important thing about saving up for your "cucumbers" is that you want to make sure that saving for purchases isn't muddled up with your savings for retirement or emergencies - otherwise you won't really know what your priorities are for your stash of money.

Where to store your funds

There are two key factors in where you want to store your savings: how "liquid" it is, and how much interest your money can earn for you. For this reason, a money market account can often offer the best "place" for your emergency fund savings. A money market account is a type of investing account that is generally low-risk because it is federally insured but provides a slightly better return than a regular savings account. They have some of the benefits typical of both savings and checking accounts.

They can offer a higher interest rate because they often have a higher minimum balance and there are usually restrictions on how much you can withdrawal per year. This makes it a great place to stash an emergency fund.

The thing about money market accounts is that usually they give you a very limited amount of checks you can write per year. There's federal regulations that limit check-writing ability on savings and money market accounts, so if you end up writing a bunch of checks out your savings account (say for a medical crisis) you could get hit with fees.

There's a few things to look for when shopping for a money market account: the interest rate it provides (this varies based on the economy, but compare against a typical savings account to see if it is higher), the minimum balance to open (often $5,000 or $10,000 but they can go as low as $1) and the minimum monthly balance - often you'll owe a fee if you dip below $500 per month.

If you're opening a joint account with your partner, it's important to make sure both you and your partner have check-writing ability and have names on the account. I've seen far too many people have the contents of joint accounts disappear off the face of the earth in a breakup because only one person was listed on the account.

CD Ladder

An alternative to a money market account is to utilize a CD ladder. CD ladders take some strategy but can yield a bit more than Money Markets are right now. CDs are certificates of deposit, which are bank accounts that are *totally locked* for a pre-approved portion of time, but give you a guaranteed rate of return. These are considered low risk as they are federally insured but your money is locked up.

So, for example, for 6 months, you couldn't touch the money without paying a penalty, but you'd earn interest on that money at end of that 6 month period. The longer a CD's term and the larger your deposit, the higher your rates.

A traditional place to "lock up" savings was to just re-renew a CD year after year. However, you can also do what's called a CD ladder. The traditional CD ladder model divides your investment evenly over five CDs, with one CD maturing each year.

If you had $20,000 to invest, you could spread out your money like this:

- $4,000 in a one-year CD
- $4,000 in a two-year CD
- $4,000 in a three-year CD
- $4,000 in a four-year CD
- $4,000 in a five-year CD

After your one-year CD matures, you can reinvest that money in a new five-year CD or you can drop that money in a money market account. CD ladders have a big downside - they are much less flexible than a money market. So you could end up paying a penalty if you needed to withdrawal the money on short notice. This makes CD ladders better for mid-term savings goals with clear timelines (like a wedding or down payment) than for your emergency fund.

Making Savings a Purriority

Just like my cat when it's time for her 4:30AM feeding - I'm about to get a little sharp with you: you can probably afford to save *something*. If you're making money, and you're not able to set aside any savings, it isn't because savings isn't possible for you. You can't save because saving and eliminating financial stress isn't enough of a *purr*iority to delay purchases. So instead you buy things with your savings dollars or maybe even go into debt to buy those things.

Savings isn't as complicated as the gravity-defying leaps cats make. The biggest "secret" to saving money is to make it your *furst purr*iority. Savings can help you buy your life back from being stressed out about money, more than any electronic gadget or restaurant meal can.

I've met many folks making decent incomes who believe they don't make a high enough income to save any money. But "enough money" is one of those things that is always a moving target - if you never start the habit of paying yourself first, more and more income won't change your behavior, because it will never seem like the right time. Your expenses will expand to 100% of your income over and over.

While I've met plenty of folks making more than median income who feel they can't save any money, I've also met plenty of folks like myself - making minimum wage and still able to save 20% or more of their income. It's rarely the case that you can't save absolutely anything. Most of us know what we need to do, where we need to cut back, to have a bit more left in our pocket each month. But if savings isn't a *purr*iority, it doesn't happen. But building up your savings is really the most important first step to getting out of that paycheck-to-paycheck panic cycle.

And it is never too late to start saving. Starting now is more important than beating yourself over all those dollars you don't know where they went.

Do it Automatically

Most banks will do free auto-transfers from your checking account to your savings account. If you really want to get sneaky, you can ask your job to split your paycheck deposit into to bank accounts (most will do this), and send your savings goal to a separate bank account before you even see it (maybe even at a different bank!)

Ask for Support From Your Litter

If you struggle with impulse control or could use an extra push towards savings, social accountability can really help. A common form of savings goals is a "savings club" or "tanda" where you join with 10 friends to save

$1,000 for each person. Let's say you want to save $1,000 for your buffer. You find 9 friends who also want to save $1,000 (for their own buffer, to start a business, or another priority). Each month for 10 months, everyone contributes $100 to one person's goal. For folks that get paid early, this acts as a non-interest loan. The social pressure here is the key: instead of putting off the idea of saving, every month you know you need to come up with $100 to bring to the savings club meeting. It's important that you trust the other 9 people in the savings club, of course, but this can be an excellent way to start saving if you struggle to do it on your own.

Taking Care of your Future Self

If you're currently living beyond your means (either living off loan money or charging more on your credit card than you can pay back each month), you're borrowing from your future self. Perhaps you generally do a good job of living within your means most months, but you can't put anything into savings, ever. Every month you're just breaking even.

One month, your transportation breaks down. Because you need it to get to work and you've already found nothing in your budget that you can cut back for savings, you have to put the repair on credit. Well, now you've lived beyond your means. You've borrowed from your future self to pay for that repair.

Now you'll have to make room in your budget to pay back that expense - likely the same amount of room you would have needed to make in order to save the money to be prepared for that expense. So you're paying back for that car repair, so you still can't afford to make room in your budget for that expenses. You're now stuck on the treadmill of debt.

But consider the alternative. You started saving $100 a month a few months ago. You cut back on a your phone bill and occasionally babysat for some extra money, and made sure you always put aside $100 each month towards your one month buffer. Now your car breaks down. Instead of having to borrow from your future self, you can "borrow" from your past self - and use that money to pay for the car repair. There's no extra interest charges.

You don't need to deal with the stress of an extra credit card bill.

That's the power of savings. Even a small bit of savings helps you sleep a little sounder.

The Power of "Fur-Get You" Money

Savings buys you one very special thing: the ability to say "fur-get you". Because having significant savings is so abnormal for the typical North American worker, you get to breathe a rarefied air of flexibility once you amass even a little pile of savings. Most Americans say if they lost their job unexpectedly, they don't know how they would pay their bills the very next month.[8] The general expectation is that you have nothing of your own to fall back on without a paycheck, and this lets bad bosses and companies take advantage of their workers.

A few years ago, I was working a very toxic high-pressure job. The office wasn't a happy or healthy place. Within months of starting, I dreaded going to work in the morning with such great apprehension that I felt physically ill. Now, I never earned great money, but this job was paying me a lot more than I needed to to cover my expenses. I was saving 59% of my income from this job. So I walked away.

Leaving a job without another one lined up is considered "risky" by nearly every career coach. This is based on the expectation that you don't have enough financial cushion to wait until another job turns up. My coworkers, who made fun of me for packing my lunch every day while they went out to eat, would complain about running out of money the week before payday. I happily ate my packed lunch because it bought me the savings and ability to walk away.

But because I had emergency savings stashed away - at that point, 18 months of expenses - I had the power to leave a toxic situation. I was able to just…walk away. That is some real Fur-get You (FU) Money.

Fur-get You Money doesn't need to be 18 months of expenses - that was the magic number for me in that situation, but it's probably different for you. It can be far less, or maybe it's far more for you. Your stash of FU money could be the $1,000 that you have stored up for a deposit when your Craigslist roommate turns out to be dangerous. Your stash of FU money could be the savings account that you use to restart your life and get out of an abusive relationship. Your stash of FU money could just be the $100 that you hide in your shoe so you can always take a taxi home if a date goes bad.

Savings can buy you flexibility even in good situations - with a stash of savings, you might be able to take advantage of a last-minute opportunity to take a once-in-a-lifetime-trip because you have the money stashed to pay for it. You might be able to say no to extra shifts at work because you want to see your daughter's Little League game. Savings has the potential to buy you all sorts of opportunities, if you only *purr*ioritize it.

Week Four Action Items

Tracking your Savings Rate

If you include pensions and retirement savings done for us by our employers, Americans save about 3.5% as of this writing - putting the average American on track for a 62 year working career. That amount is among the lowest of all countries in the world, despite the fact that we're the richest nation on earth. China has a personal savings rate of 28%, India has a savings rate of 32%, and the French save around 16% of their salary on average.[9]

One driver of this low savings rate is culture: American culture puts a high value on possessions and a low value on savings. Your neighbors and friends show off new possessions, cars, and houses in a way they don't show off their savings account balances.

I wish that a high savings rate was the new Ferrari of status symbols, but until that's true, you'll have to proactively decide to track your own savings rate.

Identify your next savings purrority

Using the cat tree of financial well-being and your own brainstorming, identify your next savings priority. Only pick one priority, not four! Here are some ideas:

- Your one month buffer
- A 3-8 month emergency fund
- A wedding fund
- A fund for a "known unknown" like a roof repair
- A down payment on a home
- To purchase a car

- To purchase a replacement laptop

Savings Rate

Income	Total Amount
Pre-tax Annual Income #1	
Pre-tax Annual Income #2	
Pre-tax Annual Income #3	
TOTAL OF ABOVE (A)	
Savings	**Total Amount Saved this Year (not total in account)**
Employer Retirement Savings (401K/ Pension/etc)	
IRA Savings	
HSA Contribution	
Cash Savings	
Mortgage Principal (not including interest or taxes)	
Other Savings	
Other Savings	
TOTAL OF ABOVE (B)	
DIVIDE B by A = C	
Multiply C by 100	YOUR SAVINGS RATE:

Discussion Questions

*These discussion questions are great if you are going through **A Cat's Guide to Money** with friends - but they're also worth having the conversation with yourself, your accountability partner, or just writing them out below.*

We get different cultural messages about how important savings are. Did you grow up in an environment where savings was important? Were you *purr*sonally inclined to save as a child?

What is your definition of Fur-get You money? Do you have a *purr*sonal amount of savings that you feel would give you more choices in life? Do you feel that you already have that amount saved?

Retir-Purr-Ment
Lazy Investing for your financial independence

Most house cats have lived a life of retirement since they were wee kittens. Without engaging in any kind of labor in exchange for money, their humans work to provide them with food, shelter, and catnip. My cat has never worked a day in her life, unless you count her nightly effort to meticulously knock every single unsecured object from the counter onto the floor. Yet she still has everything she needs to live a fulfilled life of naps, baths, and cuddles.

You, too, can get to the point where your money is able to support your life expenses without working every day. Instead of finding gullible humans to bring home your catnip, getting started with investing allows your money to do the work for you - and your money will make even more money, and you can live off its money babies.

Here's what I want you to know about investing before we dive in: it is not rocket science. It's not that hard. You can do it, I promise. And what's more, being a lazy investor is actually a great investing tactic!

To get yourself set up to start investing for your retirement, you need to set aside a few afternoons over the course of the next couple months. A lot of people hear "investing" and think it is something that only rich people do, or something they'll do later "when they are financially set up." Neither of those things are true!

Investing has become much more democratized over the past several decades, and you don't need to worry about picking individual stocks, dollar-cost averaging, or studying market trends to benefit from investing. You also don't need to be rich to get started investing. In fact, the earlier in your working life that you start setting some investment money aside, the less you need to save overall.

Compound inpurrest is magic

Compound interest is magic. Einstein called it the 8th wonder of the world. What compound interest means to you - without getting into complicated calculations - is that a small amount of money *early* is better than a lot of money later.

This is because investing is taking money and sending it out to work for you - to earn more money. When a lot of people think about saving for retirement, it feels like something they will do later. But if you start early, you can pretty much set the entire thing on autopilot and walk away.

Here's why compound interest is magic - let's look at this example of Puss, Oscar, and Tigger on the next page. Puss starts saving early - when she's 25. She's saving $5000 each year between age 25 and 35. She stops at age 35. In total, she invests $50,000 of her own dollars. Based on the average rate of return, despite only contributing for 10 years, she still ended up with over $600,000 at age 65 thanks to her dollars making more dollars for her.

Now I want you to look at her friend Tigger. Tigger put off saving for retirement until he was 35. He saved $5,000 per year, for 30 years - all the way until he was 65 years old. So he put in three times as much money as Puss - $150,000 all together.

But he ends up with less money than her despite putting in more money over a longer period of time - why? Well, because of the magic of compound interest! While he was trying to catch up to Puss, Puss had stopped contributing entirely but her dollars were working for her, making more dollars.

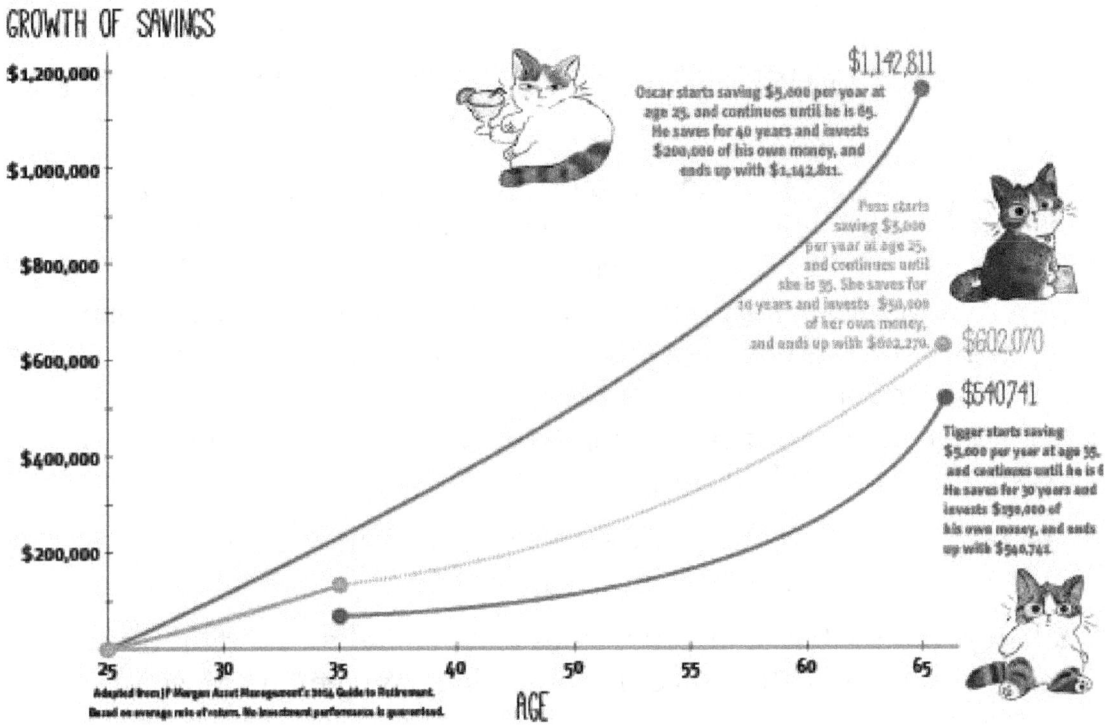

Now, let's look at our last friend Oscar. Oscar is a super-saver. He contributes $5,000 year every single year from age 25 until age 65 - starting at the same time as Puss, but never stopping. He puts in only $50,000 more than Tigger overall, but ends up with over one million dollars - twice as much - as Tigger, because he prioritized early savings (you'll notice that Oscar earned exactly as much as Puss and Tigger combined.) That's the power of compound interest.

Now, I'm not doing this to make you feel bad if you don't have this much money. I'm not doing this to make you feel bad if you're 40 years old and you haven't started saving for retirement. I'm doing this to show the power of compound interest and convince you that having your money make more money is worth it. But if you didn't start early, it's okay! You can still start saving. It's never too late - but the later you start, the more you have to save, or the longer your working career has to be while you wait for your money to compound.

There's no better time to start than right meow

I hear all the time from folks that they can't afford to save for their retirement. I've been low-income most of my working career, so I understand the struggle of finding some extra cash - I think my average annual income hovers somewhere around the $17,000 mark, which is just at poverty level for my area. But if you're young, even if you don't have a lot of money, time is really on your side when it comes to investing regardless of income. This is true even if you can't make room for a huge contribution - when it comes to long-term investing, early contributions make up for big contributions.

If you start in your twenties, just $25/month can help set you up for a comfortable, panic-free retirement plan.

I started putting $50/month in my Roth IRA (an individual retirement account) when I was 20 years old and making $800 per month as an AmeriCorps member.

$50 a month seemed like a huge amount of money at the time, but I knew that I wanted to get started early so I built it into my budget. I kept contributing to the Roth IRA all the way through college in my mid-twenties.

I never touched my Roth IRA, but I always had in the back of my head that it was a little bit of a safety net. It was never my only emergency fund, but thanks to the flexibility of the Roth IRA (compared to a 401K), I knew I could pull it out for college or an emergency if I really needed to.

That little Roth IRA lived through the recession, since most of my twenties the country's economy was doing terribly. It was hard not to panic sometimes when I watched my IRA tank as the economy was falling apart, but I would just remind myself that I'm in it for the long-haul and that there are ups and downs in the market. The best long-term investments are ones that you don't screw with too much. I knew that good investing is lazy investing.

So I didn't touch my investments beyond a few adjustments for allocations and mostly just ignored my IRA account other than putting $50 in each month. Even when I got statements showing a loss at the end of the tax year, I didn't panic and pull my money out or stop contributing. And now that the economy has mostly recovered, and my measly little $50 per month contributions stand at over $20,000 in value - nearly half of which is growth, rather than money I put in myself.

That means the money in my retirement account EARNED more money without me doing anything. Those little dollars made dollar babies.

But here's where compound interest makes a dif*fur*rence for lazy kittens. I'm thirty years old right now: if I don't contribute another cent to that Roth IRA, if I *never make* another contribution again, based on the average rate of return of 8% after inflation, I will have $500,000 by age 67. That's enough to support my current lifestyle each year without working. So, thanks to my dedication to putting aside money in my twenties, even when my income was very low and it seemed very challenging, compound interest is at work helping me out.

If you want to be a lazy millionaire, start early

Eight of ten millionaires in America are self-made, and very few have the typical "high powered jobs" like lawyer, stock broker, or doctor.[10] Most simply saving early and often. If you want to be a millionaire by age 65, here's how much you need to save each month if you have the average 8% rate of return:

- $210 per month starting at age 20
- $468 per month starting at age 30
- $1,095 per month starting at age 40
- $2,950 per month starting at age 50

Low income? Look for the savers credit

If you're low income and you put money aside for retirement, you may qualify for the Saver's Credit. The Saver's Credit is the government actually giving you back money on your taxes if you give to retirement to say "thank you for planning for your future." So that means you get a double benefit - you've put away savings for retirement, and you get cash back on your taxes. It's like an extra savings match!

One of the most important things to consider when it comes to saving on taxes when you're in lower income brackets is the difference between refundable credits versus deductions. Deductions simply reduce the amount of money you owe. If you're low income, you often don't owe much, if any, taxes, so deductions only go so far. But credits are often refundable, meaning that you can get them back as a refund if they add up to more than what you owe.

Baskets + Boxes: opening a retirement account

So you're convinced and want to start saving early. But how do you do that?

The first thing I want to talk to you about is the actual accounts where your money "lives." When people talk about having a 401K or IRA, this is what they are talking about. Your money invested for retirement can be put in a few different special types of accounts. The advantage of these accounts is that they have preferential tax treatment over just stuffing your money in a mattress or a savings account.

These accounts are also known as "vehicles". The "vehicle" for your retirement is simply the place where it is stored. There's two main kinds of vehicles, pre-tax (Traditional) and post-tax (Roth). I like to think of them as baskets and boxes.

The traditional, or pre-tax is a like a box - it's easy to get into, but it closes up and is harder to get money out of until retirement age.

The Roth is post-tax, meaning the money comes out after you pay taxes. It's sort of like a basket - more open top, meaning there are ways to access it before retirement age.

Choosing your basket or box is the first step, and your next step is choosing the actual investments to put into the basket and boxes. While there's a few differences in the amount you can put aside in each type of account, the main difference is when you pay taxes on the money you save. In the Traditional "box", the money you save is pre-tax. This means you can save more money without "feeling it" come out of your paycheck as much. For example, if you are in the 20% tax bracket, saving $100 per month in a

Traditional 401K would only "feel" like $80 per month out of your paycheck, since usually that last 20% would go to taxes.

Pre-tax retirement savings is also an excellent way to lower your overall taxable income. So if you have a higher income and have a bigger tax bracket, you can save into a Traditional "box" in order to get your overall income lower and pay less taxes. The downside is that you will have to pay regular income tax when you withdraw the money at retirement age!

Your other option is the Roth "basket" - the Roth is post-tax, which means that you save in your Roth basket after you pay regular income taxes on the income, just like you would if you saved in a savings account. But, unlike saving in a regular savings account or in cash under your mattress, your Roth will be able to grow and grow totally tax free, and you won't pay taxes on it when you withdraw it.

For most people, income is the biggest factor in selection of traditional versus Roth. If your income, and therefore the amount you pay in taxes, is lower, you most likely want a Roth. If your income, and therefore your tax burden, is higher, you most likely want Traditional.

Both the Roth basket and the Traditional box come in different flavors - either IRA (Individual Retirement Arrangement) and employer-sponsored plans like your 401K or 403B. As you can see from the Cat Tree of Financial Priorities (page 64), you can use a mix of IRAs and 401Ks.

Traditional 401K or 403B

A Traditional 401K (for some public sector or nonprofit employees, the equivalent plan is Traditional 403B) is a pre-tax retirement account provided through your employer. It's the most common form of retirement savings. You usually choose a percentage of your income to save automatically in your 401K, such as 15% or 20%. If you have a traditional job (rather than being a self-employed cat economist like me), it's possible your retirement account has a perk called *a company match*. Company matches are fantastic benefit, because they can double what you save for retirement, at no cost to you! It's free money.

401K matches are structured in many different ways at different employers, but a common match is the company will match dollar-for-dollar what you save up to a percentage (i.e. 3%) of your salary. Whatever your match is, it's like turning down a raise if you don't contribute enough to get the match - so make it a *purr*iority, even if you're still paying off debt or are doing most of your savings in an IRA.

Roth IRA

A Roth IRA is an individual retirement account that you can set up even if your employer doesn't offer a retirement plan or in addition to it. The best thing about a Roth IRA is that it is totally in your control - you can choose the investment options in it, and you don't need to worry about rolling over the account if you leave a job. This is why the Roth IRA is my recommended first retirement vehicle for most people (after contributing to the company match on their 401K).

The other unique thing about a Roth IRA is that it is flexible - after a few years, you can pull out your own contributions (but not the earnings) without penalty (of course, you won't get the benefits of long-term compound interest in that case.) You can even pull out your earnings even before you hit retirement age for things like a down payment on your first home purchase, and educational expenses. Ideally, you have other short-term savings for those things so that your Roth can grow, but it is good to know that it's more flexible than a traditional IRA or 401K. The downside of a Roth IRA is that if your income goes above a certain amount, you can't qualify for it anymore, and if you're a super-saver, it has a pretty low limit on how much you can save in it ($5,500 per year in 2018, as compared to $18,500 for the 401K.)

Traditional IRA

A Traditional IRA is an individual account that you can set up even if your employer doesn't offer a retirement plan, but instead of being post-tax like a Roth IRA, it is pre-tax. Your limit is considered with the Roth IRA - so if the annual limit for IRAs is $5,500, you can't save more than that each year between both accounts, but you could save $2,000 in your Traditional IRA and $3,500 in your Roth IRA. If you're a super-saver, you can contribute the maximum on your 401K and on your IRAs.

Roth 401K

A Roth 401K is just like a a regular 401K, except the money that is put in will be post-tax instead of pre-tax. They still aren't a very common option at most employers, but there's a few reasons you might utilize a Roth 401K if you have access to one: it's a great way to have your saving grow tax free for retirement while still getting a company match (instead of having both a 401K and a Roth IRA), or your household makes too much income to have a Roth IRA, or you'd like to save more than the Roth IRA limit.

Just like the Roth IRA and Traditional IRA, your limit for a Roth 401K is combined with your Traditional 401K. So if the limit is $18,000 for a 401K, you can save $9,000 in your Roth 401K and $9,000 in your Traditional 401K, but not $18,000 in both.

 Simple IRA

An uncommon type of retirement account is a SIMPLE IRA, which despite having "independent" in the name, is actually provided by your employer. It's nearly identical to a Traditional IRA except it has slightly higher limits and you cannot set one up on your own. One unique factor about these is that they *must* have a company contribution by law - either a dollar-for-dollar match of up to 3% of salary or a flat 2% of pay, even if you don't contribute.

Self Employed Options

If you are self-employed like me, you have a couple more options than someone with a traditional job. In the eyes of the tax authorities, you are both the *employer* and the *employee* and are able to set aside even more of your income to save for retirement. This can be really useful as a self-employed person because usually you have lots of taxes to pay - if you can save a lot of money for retirement in your special retirement accounts, you can pay less taxes overall! Your unique options are:

- **Solo 401K** - this is just like a traditional 401K, except you get to be both the employer and the employee! You can contribute up to $55,000, depending on the profit of your business.
- **SEP IRA** - this is like a Traditional IRA set up by your business for you, but the limit is much higher than a Traditional IRA - up to 25% of your business's income (or $55,000, whichever is less). These are easier to administer than Solo 401Ks.

I have a basket or box. Now what do I put into it?

Once you've started saving money into your retirement account, you need to actually invest in stocks and bonds. Likely, what will happen is you will set up the payment and then be totally confused about what things to press next! I know this is where things get scary for many folks. But we've got some kittens here to help explain it to you! You probably already know that when you buy a share of stock, you're buying a tiny piece of a company. Let's imagine that each type of cat toy is a company.

If you were to buy stock in one of these companies, you would be taking some of your money and investing a sliver of money into these companies. So buy buying stock, you will buy a portion of Sparkly Balls Ltd or Bell Balls Corporation. All these tiny bits of companies you own in your investing accounts is called your "portfolio." So, if you're investing in our world of cat toys, you might have a portfolio made up of a little bit of sparkly balls, felt mice, stick toys, and bell balls.

Sparkly Ball Ltd

Felt Mice Co

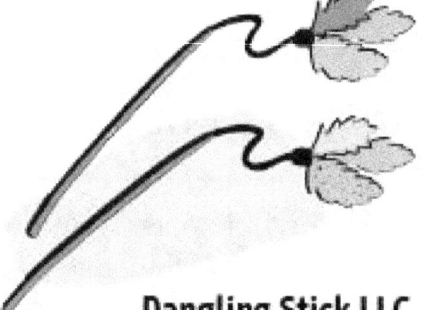
Dangling Stick LLC

Bell Ball Corporation

Diversification

As much as you personally might like sparkly balls (my cat Dora thinks they are the best and would love a portfolio made entirely of them), the safest way to invest is to invest in a lot of different types of companies. This is because you want to spread out the risk of investing (you never know if we find out that sparkly balls are toxic or a better, sparkly ball comes along produced by a different company).

Despite Dora's preferences for sparkly balls, this is an undiversified (and risky) portfolio.

Diversification is one of the key elements in building a strong retirement portfolio. This is one of the most important parts or making sure to balance your risk in investing: making sure you have a diversified portfolio, meaning a broad type of industries, company sizes, and types of investments.

You might laugh at Dora and her portfolio full of sparkly balls, but many folks do this same thing accidentally by receiving bonuses of company stock in their retirement or pension plan and never adding in any other funds. In that case, not only is your earned income (your job) tied up in one company, so are your investments! If you want to know why this is not good financial planning, ask former Enron employees.

Dora decided to diversify her Roth basket from only sparkly balls into a more balanced index fund - with a little bit of every company.

So when you're putting together your portfolio, you're looking for a good diverse mix of company sizes, industries, and locations.

This doesn't mean, however, that you need to go out an individually research every company in your portfolio. Instead, one of the easiest ways to get a good mix is to invest in something called a fund.

A fund allows you to invest in many different types of companies with one "purchase" without hunting down individual stocks.

Remember that the US isn't the only market in the world: usually you want a portion of your portfolio invested outside the United States - so that your fortune isn't only tied to one country.

Choose a fund and take a nap

One of the easiest ways to get a mix of different companies inside your portfolio is to invest in a *total market index fund* with a low expense ratio. Now, let me back up in case I've lost you because I know I just threw a lot of scary words at you.

When you own stock you own a piece of a business. The act of investing in what is called an "index fund" is sort of like tearing out the index out of the back of an encyclopedia: you get a tiny glimpse of everything. Just like the index of a book, an index fund contains an overview of everything: you'll get bad stocks, you'll get good stocks, but you'll get one single line of everything, rather than an entire page of one thing. When you own a US total market index fund you own a tiny sliver of every publicly traded business in the United States.

The great part about index funds is that we don't have to stress about if we've made the right choice in our stock picks. We're not choosing horses at a race. We bet on tiny slivers of everything, which means that we'll win a little bit. You'll do exactly as well as the US stock market as a whole, which is pretty good over the long run. The market is also "self-cleansing" like a kitty - bad companies will close up over time, and good companies will prevail. This is not only one of the best-performing wealth building investment strategies, it's also the easiest. You don't need to stress about picking stocks, which I know before I learned about this stuff is what I thought "investing" was. **You can be lazy, it's okay.**

Gizmo is a smart index fund investor - he has chosen his fund, and taken a nap instead of fiddling with all his investments.

One of the worst things you can do is panic when the market taxes a dive and pull all your money out! Ignoring your portfolio like a sleepy cat will help you avoid panic.

Index funds are not just for "lazy investors" though, they actually give the best returns overall - statistically, even professional fund managers who "actively manage" (trade stocks) do not beat the market as a whole over the long run, and when they do it's hard to distinguish luck from skill.[11] So, be like a cat - choose your spot (or index fund), and take a nap. The more you fiddle with your investments or try to pick winning stocks, the less likely that you will have success. Lazy investors who pick a fund, set it, and *fur*get it do the best in the long term. As J.L Collins, one of my favorite investing educators, says "The great irony of investing is the more you watch and fiddle with your holdings the less well you are likely to do."[12]

Where do these index funds even exist?

You've probably wondering how you go about finding an index fund. Well, you're going to login to whatever your investing provider is - this might be your 401K at work, or it could be the "brokerage" that holds your IRA. The way you look for a fund that is an index fund is look for the words "total market" or "index fund." If you'd like to get money invested outside the US, look for international index funds as well. I personally prefer a Total Stock Market Index Fund because it includes smaller companies, but one tracking the S&P 500 index (that includes the top 500 companies in the US) is also diversified.

When you're choosing funds for your portfolio, you want to keep an eye on a key statistic: the expense ratio. This is how much you're charged by the fund provider for their administration of the fund. The lower your expense ratio, the more of your own money you get to keep and let compound. The general rule is that every time a human touches your money, they will take a piece of it. The lowest expense ratio funds are managed automatically by robots (instead of humans).

On the low end, you can find expense ratios for index funds below .05%. Ideally you want something below .15% at the very least, anything higher than that can cost you tens of thousands of dollars in the long term.

If the expense ratio is not obvious on your fund selection page of your retirement account, you can search the six-letter code for your fund (VTSAX, for example) and the words "expense ratio" and you'll get back a percentage. If you have limited fund choices in your 401K, you may have to settle for a higher expense ratio.

Calvin has invested in an index fund in his Traditional 401K - he has a little bit of everything, diversifying his risk.

Allocation

There's two primary activities you want your basket of investments to support over your life: *building* your wealth and *preserving* your wealth. The distance you are from retirement age is the primary thing that determines which type of investor are in. If you're under the age of 40, you're firmly in the "wealth building" stage - far enough from retirement that you need to be more aggressive with your portfolio. There are three main "tools" that you use to achieve those goals: stocks, bonds, and cash.

The amount of your portfolio you have in stocks & bonds is called your "allocation" - a common rule of thumb is that you subtract your current age from the number 110, and that is the percentage of your portfolio that should be in stocks, and the rest should be in bonds. So a 6-week old kitten would have a high percentage of their portfolio in stocks, but an elderly kitty would have most of their portfolio in bonds. Both bonds and stocks are available in index funds, and that is the laziest way to build your portfolio.

Bonds don't usually provide as high of returns to your portfolio, but they tend to be lower risk. They provide income to your portfolio and help you hedge against deflation. But when the economy is doing really well, and there's inflation, bonds don't do as well. So you want a mix. As you get closer to retirement age, you want more bonds because they help you preserve your wealth. This means even if the market crashes right before your retirement date, you won't lose your fortune because your portfolio will be mostly bonds.

Building your portfolio

When you build your portfolio, you want to consider expense ratios, allocation, and diversification. Here is a sample DIY lazy retirement plan for a 30 year old single woman with no dependents, who makes $45,000 per year.

She saves 15% of her income for retirement - $6,750 per year ($281 per paycheck), and receives a 3% match from her employer - $1,350 per year.

- She puts 60% of her portfolio in Vanguard Total US Stock Market Index Fund because it has low expense ratios and is diversified across the whole market.
- She puts 20% of her portfolio in Vanguard Total International Stock Index Fund to spread her risk between countries.
- Puts 20% in Vanguard Total Bond Index Fund in order to provide some income and stability to her portfolio

How to rebalance your portfolio

About once a year, you want to login in and "rebalance" your portfolio. This means you "sell" your stock or bond funds in order to get back to your target percentage for your age. For example, let's say your original allocation was 60% stocks and 40% bonds. If the stocks performed well during this year, it could have increased the stock weighting of the portfolio to 70%. You would need to login and sell your stock index fund and buy more bond index fund to get the portfolio back to the original goal allocation of 60/40. This should take you about 15 minutes per year.

Target Retirement funds

One neat innovation for lazy investors out there are something called "Target Retirement Funds". These funds do rebalancing automatically based on your age. So when you're young, they will have a high allocation of stocks, but as you get closer to retirement, they will put more of your investment in stocks. So if you will turn 65 in the year 2050, your target retirement fund would be Target Retirement 2050.

Target Retirement Funds are frequently offered in your employer-sponsored plan and these can be an excellent way to be a lazy kitten who doesn't need to re-allocate their portfolio. You do want to check the expense ratios and fees on these funds because often they are higher than those for index funds. For the lowest fees, you'll look for ones made of index funds that are auto-balanced not made of actively managed mutual funds (remember, robots do better than humans at investing over the long term). Automatic retirement funds are relatively simple - they automatically adjust your stock and bond percentages as you get closer to retirement age.

Early Retire-purr-ment: not just for the rich

Many people think that early retirement is something that is only possible if you invent silent velcro or have a trust fund. But in fact, the most important factor in your ability to retire early is your savings rate, which is the percentage of your income you can save. Saving just a little bit more each month can make a huge impact on how long your working career needs to be - particularly because if you save 20% of your income instead of 10%, that means you've reduced your expenses enough to live off 80% of your total income instead of 90%. This is how savings rate has such a large effect on working career length.

Sabrina
Formerly New York, NY, now traveling the country for democracy

There are even extreme folks out there, like me, who strive for 50% or greater savings rates in order to have enough income to retire early. This is also great to track if you're getting started late with retirement savings.

This really does make a big difference over the long run! For example, a middle-class family with a $50,000 take-home pay who saves ten percent of their income - five thousand dollars - is actually doing much better than the average American, who saves only 3.5% of their income.[9] But unfortunately, "better than average" still means that they are on track to work into their seventies.

But say that they make a few lifestyle changes - they decide to get rid of cable TV or they aggressively pay off their debt - and they boost their savings rate to 15%. This would allow both income earners to retire a whole eight years earlier. How *paw*some is that?

SAVINGS RATE	YEARS TIL RETIREMENT (BASED ON INVESTING AT 8% RATE OF RETURN)
10%	51 years
15%	43 years
20%	37 years
25%	32 years
30%	28 years
40%	22 years
50%	17 years

Week Five Action Items
Start Saving

Once you've gotten your one month buffer (Chapter 4) set aside, your next step is to contribute up to the match on your 401K if you have one. Don't turn down free money! If you don't have an employer-sponsored plan, set up an IRA on your own and start putting aside $10 a month.

If you feel like there's no room in your budget to start saving for retirement, try a slow method to ramp up your savings - save 1% the next three months (I promise you won't notice very much), then move up to 2% the next three months, then 3% the next quarter. The slow increase will make this feel like less of a shock!

Discussion Questions

*These discussion questions are great if you are going through **A Cat's Guide to Money** with friends - but they're also worth having the conversation with yourself, your accountability partner, or just writing them out below.*

If you've struggled to start saving for retirement in the past, what was it that kept you from doing so? Was it not feeling like you had enough money, debt payments, feeling like you could worry about it later, or expecting someone else to do the saving for you?

Many parents struggle to *purr*ioritize their own retirement savings before saving for their kids college education. Why do you think college savings should come after retirement savings?

You've seen that small contributions add up over time and that using pre-tax retirement accounts can make the impact on your take-home pay relatively small. What do you think your biggest barrier in saving for your retirement will be?

Credit, The Great American Laser Pointer Chase

Often when I'm talking to folks about their financial well-being, they refer to their credit score. They say things like "I'm terrible with money, my credit score is awful" or "I'd really like to focus at getting better at saving and increase my credit score."

Trying to get a great credit score is sort of like a cat chasing a laser pointer: it can be fun to do, but in reality, someone else is completely in control of the pointer and your credit score - like that little red dot - changes all the time.

Here's the thing to understand about a credit score: the amount in your bank account, in your investments, your income, and many other factors about your financial health are not recorded.

Your credits scores (yes, there are more than one!) don't know very much about your financial well-being. They are simply the result of a system that is used to determine if you are a good risk to lenders. They are simply is a measure of how likely it is you'll pay back your debt. So focusing on your credit in absence of your other financial well-being goals won't get you very far. A good credit score can be part of your financial plan, or a positive side effect of executing the other parts of your financial plan, but it shouldn't be your only financial goal.

There are so many myths out there about credit and my hope is that this chapter will help you dispel some of the myths, mystique, and confusion around credit scores.

Where did this little red dot come from?

Just like kitties trying to understand a laser pointer red dot, it can be a little confusing to figure out where exactly the number on your credit scores comes from. To understand the structure of credit scores, it's helpful to learn a little about surprisingly feminist history of credit scores.

Just a few generations ago, if you wanted to borrow money to purchase a house or finance a business, you had to have a relationship with a banker or other person with wealth, and that person would look at the risk of the thing you were trying to borrow money for and would evaluate you on a personal level to determine if you were a good risk. There were no legal limits on what they could use in their evaluation of you: often banks would have thick files from private investigators that would contain your repayment history and your income - but also your religion, your club membership, your ethnicity, and maybe even details on whether or not you cheated on your spouse. They were able to use all sorts of information to decide if they wanted to lend you money.

Because of this system, the people who most often were lent money because they were considered "low risk" looked a lot like the people who already had money - white Anglo-saxon protestant men. This meant that access to building generational wealth (through building businesses or acquiring land) was rarely available to folks with different religions, ethnicities, or skin colors, and nearly all unmarried women. If a woman wanted to get a mortgage to purchase a house, most banks required that she had a man apply for the credit (i.e. her father or husband). If a woman wanted to so much as buy a vacuum cleaner, often, the store would call her husband to make sure that the purchase was okay with him. Of course, some communities set up their own banks (such as the African-American-owned United Bank, a Civil Rights-era bank intended for the movement to be able to self-finance[13]) or informal lending networks, but those options were few and far between.

In 1974, the Equal Credit Opportunity Act (ECOA) changed the way banks could make their lending decisions - now they had to disregard race, marital status, gender, religion, and many other factors. They use your credit reports (lists of all your past debt obligations and repayment history) and your credit scores. Credit scores are a numerical measure of your likeliness to repay your debt provided to banks by 3rd party agencies called credit bureaus. They were introduced as a colorblind and unbiased way to determine if someone was a good lending risk. With credit scores, the idea was that we all start at a "zero" score and our credit score will increase as we prove our trustworthiness.

There's a fair amount of evidence that credit scores and the ECOA have not accomplished the level playing field they promised[14], but they have opened the game to be played by more people. But you need to know the rules of the game, otherwise you're just chasing a dot that might disappear on you.

How does my little red dot get made?

So if we know what can't be included in a credit score, what exactly is in there? How does this little red dot even appear at all? The bad news is that the exact way that your credit score is determined is a proprietary algorithm kept secret by the credit bureaus. The good news is that we have reverse-engineered a pretty good idea what goes into your credit score.

Many people think that they have a single credit score but actually most folks have three credit scores, one from each of the credit bureaus. Even if you aren't a US citizen, if you interact with banking institutions in the US, you likely have a credit report and a score.

Each bureau has a different name for the final scoring model they use to give your a final score. The credit bureaus are Equifax (BEACON score), Experian (FICO score), and TransUnion (EMPIRICA score). Each of these bureaus get information about you reported by governments and lenders, and they compile it into a report. Not every single bureau will have the exact same set of information about you in the report, because certain banks might only report to certain bureaus. Legally, you are entitled to a copy of your report from each of the three bureaus each year. You can download them at annualcreditreport.com

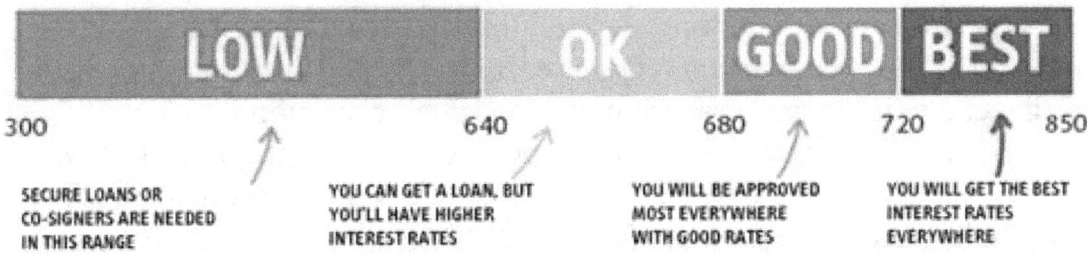

While the exact score range varies by scoring model, they all go from low scores being the worst to high scores being the best. It's easier to move up at the lower levels than it is at the higher levels - moving from a 300 to a 350 can be done in a month, but moving from a 800 to an 850 is much harder. Once your score is above ~760 or so on every model, small improvements in your score don't help much. Having an 830 credit score won't get you a better interest rate on a mortgage than a 790 credit score.

CREDIT BUREAU	SCORING MODEL	RANGE OF SCORE
Equifax	BEACON	300 - 850
Experian	FICO	340 - 820
TransUnion	EMPIRICA	150 - 934

What is in the little red dot

There's five main factors that go into your credit score: payment history, amount you owe, new credit, length of credit history, and the types of credit. They each have a different total effect on your score, represented by a percentage.

Your Payment History (35% of score)

The biggest impact of your credit score, this metrics looks at how often you have made on-time payments on your debt. If you pay your student loans, mortgage, credit cards, or car payments on time every month, this will report positive information back to the bureaus each month. If you're late on a payment, you will see a big negative effect on your credit score. The later you let it go (measured in 30, 60, and 90 days), the bigger the negative effect. The longer ago your late or missed payment was, the less of a negative effect it will have on your score.

The amount that you owe (30% of Score)

The more you owe, the lower your credit score will be, generally, because lenders will be concerned you will pay everyone else before them. However, the amount you owe is also measured in "utilization" - so if you have a $10,000 credit limit on a credit card, but only owe $500 on it, you will have a utilization percentage of 5% - which is considered good. Ideally, the credit bureaus prefer a utilization of below 30%.

Length of your credit history (15% of Score)

Credit bureaus like to see a long credit history, and they usually judge by the average age of your accounts taken together. This is why it's often best to keep your oldest credit card open (to lengthen the average age of credit). When you're just getting started out with the US credit system, this will be low.

New credit (10% of score)

When you apply for new credit and your credit gets pulled, the credit bureaus will put a small "ding" (a 10-15 point drop) in your score for about 90 days. This is because if you're applying for a bunch of new credit, it could be a red flag to lenders that you're over-extended. If you're shopping for a mortgage lender or an auto loan within a week or so of one another, usually the credit bureaus will group these inquires together into one small ding (so that you can compare lenders!) Usually this ding recovers after 90 days.

Mix of Credit (10% of Score)

The credit bureaus reward a "mix" of different types of credit - they like to see mortgages, credit cards, student loans, etc. However, this metric is a small percentage of your overall score, and you should not use this as a reason to take out more debt! I have only ever had credit cards (that I pay off every month) and my credit score is over 800.

Notice that all those metrics have to do with debt. If you have always lived debt-free, you will not have a credit report or score. Traditional forms of financial responsibility - like paying your utilities and rent on time - are usually not reported as positive information, only negative. So even if you've paid your rent and electricity bill on time, every time, for the past decade, it won't show up in your credit report.

If you want to have a credit report and score, you'll need to take out some form of "debt instrument" in order to start building a history with the credit bureaus. Usually this takes the form of a credit card, which if you pay off every single month, will allow you to build a credit history without paying any interest.

If credit isn't impurrtant, why worry?

Many personal finance experts who are anti-debt will tell you not to worry at all about your credit, and simply let your score go to zero by closing all your credit accounts. They say that if you focus on saving and don't take out debt, you don't need a good credit score. There's plenty of credence to this argument, especially if you've had trouble with past.

> **WHY YOUR CREDIT SCORE CAN MATTER**
> - Can help or hurt you getting an apartment
> - Insurance rates can be determined by credit
> - Can be used to evaluate you for jobs or security clearance
> - Can allow you to rent a car
> - Can determine if you can get a contract mobile phone
> - Medical procedures not covered by insurance (LASIK, top surgery)
> - Utility companies might require a deposit with low credit
> - And the obvious: mortgages, business, and car loans

It's *purr*fectly possible to live without a good credit score. A credit score is not a measure of your financial health. You can have healthy savings, a retirement account, a good job, and a terrible credit score. In fact, if you've never taken out debt and never lived above your means, you may have no credit score at all, despite having a relatively financially healthy lifestyle.

I have a friend Michael who managed to go to college without ever taking out student loans, thanks to some help from family and a scholarship. While he was in college he worked as a bartender and saved all his tips in cash as his emergency fund.

He kept working in bars after college, and actually had amassed quite a lot of cash - that he kept mainly in a shoebox, but some of it in his local credit union - by his late twenties. He eventually got a white collar job, but still kept up catering gigs on the occasional weekend, not wanting to lose his cocktail-making skills. He actually was doing pretty financially well - at some point, he opened a Roth IRA since their was no 401K at work, and he made sure to put aside $100 per month for retirement. By the time he turned 32 last year, he was making around $45,000 per year plus a few hundred a month from his side gig, had about $20,000 in his retirement account and a pretty hefty emergency fund in cash and in savings at his credit union. He was financially well.

But he was a ghost to the credit bureaus because he paid for everything in cash and had never taken out debt. He didn't show up in credit searches at all - he was what is called "credit invisible" (just like that laser red dot when the laser pointer is turned off.) Being credit invisible isn't bad for your finances by itself - it was fine until Michael and his boyfriend wanted to rent an apartment together in Chicago. Chicago is a notoriously tight rental market - his boyfriend had $15,000 in student loans and a low credit score. They had trouble finding any landlord that was willing to rent to them. This was despite offering an extra deposit paid in cash and past landlord references. They eventually found an apartment by using a pre-approved rental screening service, but it was not in the best neighborhood. Michael decided it was probably time to start building up a credit history so that he wasn't as limited in his choices next time they wanted to rent a place.

Good or decent credit can be useful for situations just like these. If you want to improve your credit, that's great, but work to identify the underlying reason why you want to build your credit up: perhaps you've had trouble qualifying for an apartment in the past like Michael. Perhaps you would like to buy a house, finance a car, get surgery not covered by your health insurance (like LASIK or gender-reaffirming surgery), rent a car, or simply do not want to be rejected for jobs when you fail to have a credit score. But you shouldn't focus on improving your credit to the detriment of financial wellness in other - more tangible - areas.

How to fix No or bad credit

So what do you do if you don't have a little red dot at all - or you have a bad credit score from past mistakes? The first thing to remember is that having bad credit does not make you a bad person. It doesn't make you a failure - it might not even mean that you're not financially well. If you focus on shame and guilt over your credit score, you are going to feel so crappy about this that you won't get much done. So let that go. Whatever decisions you, your parent or your spouse made in the past are not what we're focusing on. We're focusing on Future You, not Past You.

A word of caution: if you don't yet have a one-month buffer in savings, you need to focus on that before you get into any aggressive credit repair or building. Your savings is the basis of your financial health cat tree and is what helps you through tough times - not credit cards or loans. Your savings is your secret weapon, so I want you to focus on that before you tackle anything else. If your bank account would be negative if your next pay check didn't show up on time, then you need to focus on savings - which could be boosting your income a bit, selling something you own, or reducing expenses - before you tackle your credit.

If you are in a position where you haven't been able to get ahead in years despite earning okay money, then you need to get on a budget and start saving before you focus on playing the credit game.

All of these credit repair tactics rely on you having some financial health before you start. If you have $300 to your name and your $800 rent is due next week, you are not financially well yet, and you should focus on the basics before you worry about that little red dot. It's like when my cat tries to chase the laser pointer when she's precariously balanced on the back of a chair - she's probably going to fall off before she gets the dot.

The first thing you need to know where you stand. Get a copy of your credit report from all three bureaus - from annualcreditreport.com. It can be tough to read credit reports since they're essentially written in financial hieroglyphs, so you also want to know your score. You can get your actual credit score from multiple places - Discover lets anyone get a free FICO score without applying for a card, and creditkarma.com and creditsesame.com are two businesses that let you look at your credit score for free.

A common myth is that checking your own credit will "ding it" (cause it to drop by a few points), but checking your own credit will not lower your score, as it is considered a "soft inquiry". Only applying for new credit will ding your credit. Even if you have good credit, you should check your credit report at least once a year in order to check for errors or fraud. This is especially true after the large 2017 credit bureau data hack, because many more people are at risk for identity theft.

If you'd like to build your credit, you have a couple options: pay back debt you owe and make good on your outstanding obligations, take out new credit and pay it back on time, every time, and last but not even remotely least: start reporting things you already do well.

The Making Good Model

If you need to clear up outstanding issues on your credit, you must talk to the creditor. This might involve some unpleasant phone calls, so make sure you find a way to make it better for yourself (take the calls in a nice park with a good beverage, or while wearing bathrobe while covered in kittens in a fluffy bed).

If you had a period of late or missing payments in the past but now pay on time, send a letter to the credit to update the report on your account. You can do this by sending a polite letter asking that the negative information be deleted and replaced with your new payment record.

If you have past due accounts, you need to get the account up to date. That does not mean you necessarily need to pay it off entirely in one go, but you need to start making payments on time, every time. (If it is a student loan, read about student loan rehabilitation in Chapter 3).

If you have delinquent accounts that have defaulted or gone to collections, you may be able to negotiate a change in your report. You can ask the creditor to accept a payoff - a portion of the debt - in exchange for erasing negative information about the account.

If your account has gone to collections, they are most likely to accept partial payment because they bought your debt from your original creditor at a discount. But if you don't have the funds to back up a promise to pay in full, don't do this. Don't offer $2,000 to pay off an account if you don't have $2,000 available to pay it off. Breaking a promise to a collections agency can cause a world of trouble for you.

Once you've started committed to making good on your bad accounts, the important thing you can do is pay on time, every single time. So make sure you set up systems that will support that for you - such as following a budget, setting up automatic payment, and freezing your credit cards in ice so you don't overcharge on them. Your credit will not recover from paying off past accounts if you don't also pay your existing debt on time, every time. **Paying on time, every time is the most important strategy for improving your credit score.**

The New Credit Model

You can take out a new line of credit and start building positive payment history to improve your credit score. If you have bad credit or no credit history at all, often the type of card you can qualify for is a "secured" credit card. These are usually available from a local bank or credit union.

You will put a set amount (usually $100-$500) in a savings account and that will be your credit limit on your credit card. You won't have access to that saving account while you have the card, because that will be the collateral for the bank in case you don't pay. For a set time period (usually 6 months or 1 year), you will use the card and pay it off on full each month. At the end of that time period, you will have positive payment history on your credit report and you will also have a mini-emergency fund in the card's savings account. The goal of the secured card is to improve your credit score enough that you're able to apply for an unsecured (normal) credit card.

There are many online services that will help you to estimate your likelihood of getting approved for different credit cards. Usually when you're starting out with building credit, you want to look for a card that has no annual fee. Most of the cards with fancy perks like airline benefits aren't going to approve you until you have a higher credit score. If you're not going to hold on debt on the card, you don't need to worry about the card's APR (Annualized Percentage Rate) at all because you won't pay interest.

If you are taking out a credit card to build your credit but you've had impulse control issues in the past, you may want to set up the card to have a small automatic transaction - like a Netflix subscription each month - and set the card up on autopayment, and then cut up or freeze the card in ice. You don't want to take out a card to improve your credit only to take out more debt you can't afford to pay back. Remember, a credit card isn't free money, it's just a different way to pay!

Reporting Good information

If you're trying to improve your credit score, you can also try to get good financial habits that you're already following reported to the credit bureaus. Remember, your rent and utility payments usually don't show up on your credit report. One way to do this is to ask your landlord to report your rent payments to the credit bureau. You can also use a third-party service that will report your utility and rent payments to the credit bureaus for a small monthly fee. While you should be cautious while researching these services, some of these services are good ways to build your credit score without taking out more debt.

Caution Kitten: Quick Fixes

Late night cable TV commercials and newspaper ads are filled with the lofty promises of credit repair services. Most of these services are simply third parties that will charge you a fee to do the exact same thing you can do on your own. If it seems too good to be true, it probably is. The most important thing to repair your credit is to pay back what you owe, on time, every time. There's no quick fixes.

If You've Got Great Credit

If you've already got credit in the "good" range, there's a couple strategies you can use to improve kick your score up a few points:

- Pay off your credit cards on a weekly basis, or before the statement date (not the due date) each month. This means your "utilization" will report as 0% to the credit bureaus, which will help improve your score.

- Keep your oldest card open. If it charges a fee, ask to move it to a no fee card (you can negotiate with credit card companies!)

- Always accept an increase in your line of credit if it is offered - but don't use it! Having more available credit will increase your available credit and lower your utilization, which improves your score.

- If your income goes up, report it to your credit card issuer (usually there is a "profile" section of their website where this information exists). If you've been a good customer, they will often increase your limit when your income increases.

If you find an error on your credit report

Errors happen frequently on credit reports, because the credit bureaus are moving so much data around. This is even more likely to happen if you have a common name. If you find an error on your credit report(s), follow these steps:

Report to Credit Bureaus All credit bureaus have numbers you can call to report errors and fraud. It's always best to follow up with mailed documentation. You may have to mail in documentation to prove the error (for example if you have someone else's information on your account, or a paid off account is reported as open).

Contact Creditors: Always mail disputes about errors directly to the creditors, enclosing a copy of your credit report.

File a police report (if identity theft) If the error is in fact fraud (someone taking out credit in your name), file a police report and report to the hotline for identity theft run by the Federal Trade Commission 1-877-IDTHEFT. You may want to "freeze" your credit when the error is resolved, preventing anyone from opening new credit on your account (including yourself until you unfreeze it.)

Credit Myths

Myth: Don't get a credit card, just use a debit card or prepaid card.

Reality: Debit or pre-paid cards do not help your credit.

Myth: Carrying a credit card balance helps your credit.

Reality: Carrying a balance actually hurts your credit. The most important thing you can do is pay your credit card bill off in full *on time, every time.*

Myth: Credit doesn't matter if you don't want to buy house or car.

Reality: There are a number of things a credit score can influence - including jobs, renting apartments, and getting a mobile phone contract.

Myth: Immigrants can't have credit scores.

Reality: You don't need to be a citizen to build a credit score - you just need to have a relationship with a US banking institution.

Myth: Opening a new credit card will hurt your score.

Reality: Usually applying for a new credit card will hurt your score temporarily (for 90 days) but the increase in available credit will usually increase your score overall.

Myth: You need a credit score to get a mortgage.

Reality: If you are willing to look around for lenders, you can get approved for "manual underwriting" instead of a credit score if you're otherwise financially responsible.

Myth: A 0% credit card is an emergency fund.

Reality: A 0% credit card should not be used as an emergency fund. Nothing compares to cash savings as an emergency fund.

Myth: It's best to have one credit card at a time.

Reality: The scoring models reward more than one card - they prefer to see three cards, if possible. But if you can only keep track of one, don't add more!

Myth: Never take a credit limit increase.

Reality: Credit limit increases (as long as you don't view them as free money) actually help your credit score because they lower your utilization.

Myth: You should finance a car in order to build credit.

Financing a car might help your credit if you have no history, but there's no reason to take out debt unnecessarily - especially if it causes you to buy more car than you would in cash.

Week Six Action Items

Fill in Your in-depth budget

Now that you've been using your kitten budget for a month (hopefully), it's time to move into more comprehensive budgeting. In the appendix, you will find an in-depth budget. Take 45 minutes this week to update your kitten budget to the in-depth budget for the next month, involving your partner if possible.

Look up your credit report

Head over to annualcreditreport.com and try to download your credit report - just choose one of the three agencies at random. If one doesn't turn up and you are young or new to the US, you might not have a report, so don't worry! Make sure you go to *annualcreditreport.com* only because there's a number of scam websites that will try to trap you into paying for your credit report or stealing your information.

Note: the website will likely ask you a trick question to verify your identity- for example if you were born in 1990, it might ask you what bank you had a mortgage with in 1992. Answer "none of the above" whenever it applies.

Discussion Questions

*These discussion questions are great if you are going through **A Cat's Guide to Money** with friends - but they're also worth having the conversation with yourself, your accountability partner, or just writing them out below.*

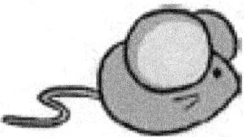

In this chapter we learned how a credit score is not a measure of financial well-being. Why do you think having a good credit score is or isn't important?

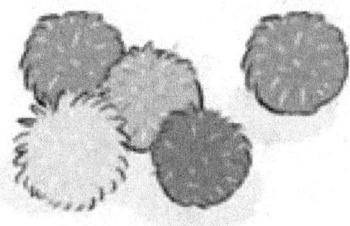

There are a lot of myths out there about the credit score. What things did you believe about credit scores that you learned in this chapter were not true?

Why do you think you shouldn't apply for a car loan to improve your credit score?

Building Your Fort
The Basics of Homeownership

Homeownership has been sold as part of the great American dream. Owning a home can be a core part of your savings and wealth-building plan, but the 2007 economy crash collectively taught us that your home should not be the core of your investment plan. *Fur*st and foremost, a house is a place to live. If too much of your wealth (and your monthly expenses) are tied up in a mortgage, you can end up in a situation where the house is a drain on your life, rather than a *paw*some part of your budget.

There are many factors that go into the decision to buy a house - the local market, your *purr*sonal priorities and your financial well-being. We can't cover all of them, so I'll just give you an overview of some of the basics of homeownership and getting financed for a mortgage. And *purr*haps, one day you too can own your own kitty castle.

Rent Vs Buy

Neither buying or renting is inherently better. They both have upsides and downsides. Here's a small list of some of the considerations for each.

RENT	BUY
• Rent payments could be lower (especially if utilities are included), giving you more money to save and invest in other ways.	• Often your monthly payment will be higher than comparable rent.
• It is easy to move or change housing if you have bad neighbors, get relocated for work, or otherwise your house isn't working for you anymore.	• Repairs are your own responsibility and must be fixed or they will cause bigger problems later.
• Your housing costs are set by the landlord, and might go up sharply (depending on local laws).	• Over time you build equity, which is ownership in the property that will turn into cash when you sell.
• If your landlord sells the property, you may have to move.	• If you need to move, it can be challenging to sell the house and you're stuck with the monthly payment until you can sell it.
• You may be restricted in how you can modify and adapt your housing.	• Owning a home means that some of your savings is locked up in a fixed asset.
• You may have restrictions on pets or vehicle parking.	• As an investment, homes are undiversified – their fate is tied to a single block, neighborhood, and city.
• Rent payments usually are not reported to credit agencies (mortgage payments are).	• You can't be kicked out of your home if you pay your mortgage and taxes.
	• Stabilizes your monthly housing costs more than rent.

How much house you can afford?

The most important factor in purchasing your home is your own budget, but lenders will approve you for a mortgage using the formula below.

1. Total Gross (Before Tax) Monthly Income	
2. Total Gross Monthly Income x .43 (43%) THIS IS YOUR DEBT-TO-INCOME RATIO	
3. Total Monthly Debt Payments INCLUDING CREDIT CARDS, STUDENT LOANS, AND CARS	
4. Subtract Line 3 from Line 2 THIS IS YOUR MAXIMUM HOUSE PAYMENT (PITI)	
5. Multiply Line 4 by .15 (15%) THIS IS YOUR ESTIMATED TAXES AND INSURANCE	
6. Subtract Line 5 from Line 4 THIS IS YOUR MAXIMUM PRINCIPAL AND INTEREST PAYMENT	
7. Divide Line 6 by Factor ($4.77 for 4% rate) GET THE FACTOR FROM THE BELOW TABLE OR YOUR LENDER	
8. Multiple line 7 by $1,000 THIS IS YOUR MAXIMUM LOAN AMOUNT	

INTEREST RATE (%)	15-YEAR LOAN	30-YEAR LOAN
3.0%	$6.91	$4.22
3.5%	$7.15	$4.49
4.0%	$7.40	$4.77
4.5%	$7.65	$5.07
5.0%	$7.91	$5.37
5.5%	$8.18	$5.68
6.0%	$8.44	$6.00

What if there's no amount of house I can afford?

A few years ago, my mid-sized city of Portland, Oregon, went through a huge population boom and suddenly our once-affordable housing skyrocketed. Normal family homes were going for over half a million dollars, while wages hadn't risen at the same rate.

Here's the thing: it's possible that with your current income or debt load, financing a home by yourself doesn't make a ton of sense for you right *meow*. Do not get pressured into buying a home just because someone told you ***it's the right thing to do.*** Make sure you're truly ready to make a six figure financial commitment and deal with the headaches of owning a home.

If you get married or have a kid, quite often people will start asking "when are you going to buy a house?" But know that kids can be raised in rentals. It's completely possible to raise a healthy, happy kid in a rental. Do not buy into the myth that the only way to take care of your family is to own a home.

> **CREATIVE HOMES**
> - A co-housing, co-op, or co-living community where there are lower land costs (and neighbors!)
> - Houseboats (most pay low or no property tax)
> - Owner financing with a third-party financial trustee
> - A land trust house where you own only the structure, not the land
> - A foreclosure or short-sale home where you buy for lower than appraised value

If you'd like to own a home for other reasons, that's fine. But don't let social pressure goad or shame or guilt about you into making an imprudent financial decision.

If you decide that you really are excited about buying a home (perhaps security is a core value) even if the numbers are working against your favor, now is time to get creative: are you willing to have a longer commute, move cities, move to a co-op or co-housing community, or get a fixer-upper?

You might be able to combine forces with another household to buy a house, but be aware that in the case of borrowing with another family, any unpaid debts (like liens or bankruptcies) they hold other than the house could put your housing at risk. In the case of one person wanting to sell the house, you may not be able to "buy out" the other party. It's important to have good legal agreements in place if buying with another family or individual.

Combining forces with another household could increase your purrchasing power, but you need to make sure everyone is aware of the risks and legal documentation is clear.

If you're low- to median-income, there are likely resources in your area that are devoted to helping you achieve homeownership, such as Individual Development Accounts (a type of matched savings account), land trust houses (where you own the home, but the land trust owns the land, lowering the cost of the home), or down payment assistance or tax abatement programs designed to lower the monthly cost of owning a home for you. The place to find a list of these programs is your local "HUD-approved Housing Counseling Agency."

Building Equity and Savings

When you purchase a home with a mortgage (as opposed to in cash), your monthly payment is usually covering three things: the principal, the interest, and taxes. (It's possible that your insurance is also part of your mortgage payment.) Your insurance, tax, and interests costs are all fees that you pay, but your principal is savings. This is the key difference between owning a home and renting. Renting does not help you build equity.

Owning a home is an excellent way to increase your savings rate, because the amount that you put towards your principal (not interest or insurance) will increase the amount of *equity* you own in the house. Your equity will also increase if the value of the home rises. Mortgages are *amortized* which means that in the beginning of your mortgage, you will be contributing a higher percentage of your monthly payment to interest, and as you get closer to the end of your mortgage, you will pay more towards the principal. That equity, while not as liquid (easy to get to) as cash savings or investments in index funds, will be available when you sell the house. You then can use that equity to purchase another home or simply as cash savings.

Some people borrow against their house equity with Home Equity Lines of Credit, but that's a risky business. Your house should not be viewed as an ATM, because if you are unable to repay your debt, you may not have anywhere to live.

Why 20% is a magic number

You've probably heard that the best down payment - the amount of cash you pay to the lender when you acquire a mortgage - is twenty percent of the home value. There are many types of financing that will allow you to put less than twenty percent down (even 0%) but any time you pay less than that, you'll pay higher fees on the mortgage, either in the form of higher interest rates or paying Private Mortgage Insurance (PMI) which is a monthly insurance fee which protects lenders. PMI can really add up, as it's usually 1% of the home loan amount each year. As soon as the amount of equity you have in the mortgage hits twenty percent (20%) you will be able to stop paying PMI.

If you can't get at least ten percent of a home price saved up, you might not be financially ready to buy, because if something unexpected happened to your income or your house, you may not have the savings to protect your home from foreclosure.

When is the time to buy

A lot of people will tell you that the perfect time to buy a home is when you're 25 - or 30, or 35, or ***right meow*** because the market is so good or because the interest rates are low.

The most important thing you should know is that the best time to buy a home is when you are *purr*sonally ready. Absolutely nothing else matters if you're not yet ready to buy a house or if you're not interested in the responsibilities of owning a home. If you buy a house not as a speculative investment or a social obligation, but instead as a place to live and as a long-term investment, it's more important to know if you can afford the home and actually want to live there than anything else. There's four key factors:

- You can comfortably afford the monthly payment, included expected increases in insurance and taxes.
- You have enough emergency savings to cover unexpected expenses, like appliance and roof repairs.
- You are planning to live in the area you're purchasing in for at least three years and would be comfortable in the home for that amount of time (i.e. you're not getting a studio apartment when you plan to have several kids in the next few years).
- You are actually interested in owning a home, including the work of fixing appliances or hiring someone to do it, and planning for future repairs and maintenance.

Are you ready to purrchase a home?

If you're not sure if getting a home is the right leap for you, this is a list of things you can use to assess your own readiness.

You have steady income in the same field for at least 2 years (if self-employed, 3 years of consistent net income).

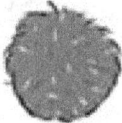

You have an annual household income of at least $30,000 per year.

You have created a budget and know how much house payment you can afford while still saving for retirement.

You have money saved for a down payment and closing costs.

Your credit score is in the "good" or "excellent" range *or* you have documented records of payments to landlords or utility companies.

You have a three month emergency fund saved separate from your down payment.

You feel ready to care for a home (and ***actually*** want to own one!)

Your monthly debt is low enough to not to limit your ability to qualify for a mortgage.

Types of Mortgages

15 year mortgage

This mortgage will have a higher monthly payment than a 30-year mortgage, but you will be 100% mortgage-free a whole 15 years earlier and you will pay lower fees and usually get a lower interest rate. If it's an affordable monthly payment to you, this will cost you the least over the long term. Many people tell themselves that they will get a 30-year mortgage and pay it off early, but few manage to make the higher payments without a mortgage in place.

30 year mortgage

This mortgage will have a lower monthly payment than a 15-year mortgage, but you will pay a lot more in interest over the life of the loan and will have your mortgage longer. (so you'll just be paying the bank more, not gaining more equity!) You'll also pay a slightly higher interest rate.

Adjustable vs Fixed Rate

An Adjustable Rate Mortgage (ARM) will change the interest rate multiple times over the life of the loan. Many people get into ARM mortgages convincing themselves they'll refinance before the interest rate gets too high. But in reality, these are usually risky bets. A fixed-rate mortgage will lock in the interest rate for the life of the loan and are much safer.

Steps in the Home Buying Process

1. Create your budget and determine what you can afford

Aim for a monthly housing cost (mortgage, property tax, insurance) of less than 33% of your monthly income.

2. Fix any issues with your credit score

You'll qualify for the best interest rates if your credit score is in the "good" or "excellent" range. If you don't have a credit score at all, you will need to find a lender who does "manual underwriting."

3. Save up for a down payment & Closing costs

Ideally, you want to aim for a 20% down payment on the *purr*chase price, which will help you avoid paying extra monthly mortgage fees. But in costly real estate markets, a lower down payment of 5% - 10% might be necessary. You don't want to have nothing in the bank after you close, so your emergency fund should not be the same as your down payment fund. Some lenders will require 3 month's expenses saved on top of your down payment.

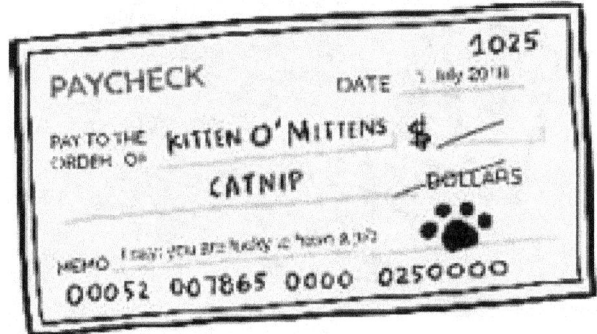

4. Get mortgage pre-approval

Many sellers now require you have a pre-approval letter to put in an offer.

To find a mortgage, ask a loan officer at your bank or credit union, or go with a mortgage broker who can shop around at multiple banks. You will need to bring in your pay stubs, bank account statements, and they will pull your credit report. You'll probably have a few different mortgage options, with different interest rates and repayment terms. Make sure you check for special programs (like down payment assistant and tax abatement) you might qualify for based on location or income.

5. Find a realtor & shop

For a first time home purchase, it's always smart to get a realtor because they'll be your advocate during the sale process and walk you through it. A good realtor is experienced and knows what to look out for. Shopping for a home can take a long time, depending on the market, so be patient. Don't rush into a six-figure purchase!

6. Make an offer

Your realtor will help you put in your offer. Your first offer(s) might not get accepted. Don't dispair if it takes awhile!

7. Sign purrchase agreement & put down earnest money

Once you have an offer accepted, you'll put down earnest money (1-2% of price) and will sign a purchase agreement.

8. Get a Loan Disclosure

You're about to get a lot of paperwork from your lender. The first of these is something called the "Truth-In-Lending Disclosure Statement" which will spell out the financial terms of your loan.

9. Get a professional home inspection

A professional home inspection is a form of insurance on your purchase - you can use what is found to negotiate on the home price or terms. Sometimes things found during inspection will cause the deal to fall through if you or your lender determines the risk isn't worth it.

10. Loan Processing & Appraisal

After you negotiate repairs, your loan processor will set up an appraisal (valuation) for the house and will review to make sure there are no liens on the property or other considerations. If they approve it, you will make the final deposit.

10. Closing

The title company will send signed loan documents to your lender. The lender will wire money to the title company. After the sale is recorded, you will get the keys and the house is yours!

For the non-standardly employed or pawtnered

Mortgage lending is still frustratingly old-fashioned in its ideas about what "stable" jobs and "normal" relationships are. If you are primarily self-employed or run your own business, you will find it that getting approved for a mortgage is a bigger hassle than it is for people with a corporate employer. If you're used to writing off many business expenses in order to lower your taxable income, you may be surprised to find that mortgage lenders only look at your income after expenses (your profit) rather than your gross income.

If you are self-employed and considering buying a first home, the amount that you have available for a down payment will factor heavily into most lender's decisions. If you have variable income but a lot of down payment money available - even more than 20 percent - you are more likely to get approved.

If you are purchasing with a *paw*tner who you are not married to legally, you will need to find a mortgage broker who is willing to do tenants-in-common financing. Usually each of you will need to have enough income to qualify for the loan on your own (married couples get their income counted together as a household), but if you have a large down payment or stable employment history, you can probably find a lender who will take you on, but you may have to look at multiple places.

Week Seven Action Item

Determine Your Net Worth

In the appendix, you will find a net worth worksheet. Take 20 minutes this week to update your assets and liabilities and find your net worth. Tracking your net worth over the long-term can help you keep an eye on your overall financial health.

Discussion Questions

*These discussion questions are great if you are going through **A Cat's Guide to Money** with friends - but they're also worth having the conversation with yourself, your accountability partner, or just writing them out below.*

Examine your housing category in your in-depth budget. What percentage of your take-home pay are you spending on housing? Do you feel that percentage is sustainable?

Many people fall into extreme camps with renting vs buying. When do you feel it is appropriate to rent? In what situation do you feel it is appropriate to buy a home?

Many people rush into buying a home when they can't afford it yet. Why do you think some people buy a home before they are ready? Have you felt pressured to buy a home by peers or family members before you were ready?

Getting Under the Umbrella
Insurance

Insurance. No one really loves spending money on insurance - even the people who make their money selling it. The hardest part of buying insurance is that you're paying for something that you hope you never have to use. Insurance isn't tangible like groceries or a new shirt. It's hard to *purr*oritize. But it's an important part of building a full financial plan.

Now, there's a bunch of ridiculous types of insurance out there that are meant to prey on the poor or financially insolvent - or the uninformed middle class. There are traps and gimmicks out there that will have you buying insurance that doesn't help you out at all, and is just meant to make money for big companies. There are only five types of insurance you will probably need:

1. Homeowner's or Renter's insurance

2. Health Insurance

3. Auto insurance

4. Disability insurance

5. Life insurance

The goal of insurance is to transfer risk for big, expensive things. You want the insurance company, instead of you, to be on the hook for really expensive misfortunes that could happen to you - large car wrecks, major illness, or death. There's a reason that the symbol for insurance is an umbrella - it's protecting you from the big downpours.

But for the little things - say a small possession being stolen or a regular doctor check up - your emergency fund and your sinking funds are your protection. These are just small sprinkles, and a rain jacket instead of umbrella will do. You want insurance for the big downpours in life - cancer or a massive car pile-up or a sudden disability. Your goal is to get insurance the doesn't cost you a ton, but protects you from life's monsoons.

Homeowner, Rental and Auto Insurance

Homeowner and renter's insurance are often requirements as part of your house financing or renting from your landlord, and auto insurance is legally required in every state for your car. So these are often the only kind of insurance that folks have by default. All three are pretty similar in structure so we'll look at them together.

When understanding the effect of insurance on your budget, the most important terms to know are premium and deductible. Your premium is what it costs you to keep the insurance, regardless of whether or not you use it. You'll pay this premium semi-annually or annually, or as part of your monthly mortgage payment.

Your deductible is the portion of the costs you will cover before your insurance company will pay out. A lot of people go for a low-premium coverage if they don't have extra room in their budget. However, paying a slightly higher premium is helpful if you don't have a lot in savings, because you can't necessarily come up with a big deductible. But as you get your emergency fund in place, raising your deductible is a good way to lower your monthly costs.

The mechanics are pretty simple: a lower premium means a higher deductible. If you have an emergency fund in place, you will save money by having a lower premium and a higher deductible. I generally recommend a deductible of around $1,000. I know that is a ton of money if you don't have an emergency fund, which is why I want you to prioritize getting that in place as your one-month buffer. In this case, your savings is actually saving you even more money, because you can afford a higher deductible.

Having a higher deductible means you can't make claims for small things like a stolen purse (unless you had $1,500 in cash in your purse). But you want coverage for the big things, not tiny things. Big umbrella, not a rain coat.

One of the ways to calculate if a higher deductible makes sense for you is to do a break-even analysis.

If your premiums go down by $75 a year, but raise your deductible by $750, then you need to go 10 years before something that would be covered by insurance happens. This isn't a super great deal, right,? Because the chances of a small car crash in 10 years is statistically high.

But if you save $500 in insurance premiums by raising your deductible $750, it only takes 1.5 years for you to break-even, which makes sense for many folks (it depends on your driving habits!) This is why running a break-even analysis is important when deciding coverage levels for your budget.

If you're in a state where it is legal to go without collision insurance, and your car is older, it's worth looking at a break-even analysis on collision insurance on your car. If your car has a low value, it's possible that it is not worth covering with collision insurance, and dropping it can save you money. Now, obviously, this is another place where having an emergency fund in place is important because you don't want to have no car

Auto insurance policies are represented by three numbers written like this:

100/300/100

In the above example, the 100 is the most the insurance company - in thousands of dollars - will pay per person for a bodily injury.

So in this example, there's $100,000 of coverage per person.

The second number is bodily injury per crash. This is the maximum combined amount that your insurance will pay for any one crash in thousands of dollars, so that means this policy covers $300,000 total per crash. The last number is property damage. In this case, the maximum they will cover to repair or replace cars injured is $100,000.

When you're hunting for coverage for homeowner's, auto, or renter's insurance, make sure you get liability coverage - this is because if you're at fault in a car crash, or if someone else gets injured at your home, this is what protects you from a massive bill - you want to aim for around $500,000 in coverage. This is because the American court system is expensive, and if you hit a BMW and someone needs to get transported to a hospital by helicopter, you'll hit a lower coverage cap very quickly.

Both homeowner's and renter's insurance protect your belongings - usually in *and* out of the house, including situations where something like a bicycle gets stolen outside a cafe. You should check what the maximum coverage per item is when shopping for insurance. Ideally, you want to look for replacement coverage - that means the insurance company will cover what it costs to replace the belonging, not what the item is worth. For example, you have a nice cat tree that was state-of-the-feline-art when you bought it, but has gone down in resale value in the past several years thanks to your cats scratching it daily. If that cat tree was stolen, and you don't have replacement coverage, you'll only get a check for what the cat tree is worth - but if you have replacement coverage, you will get a check for what it costs to go to the store and buy a new cat tree.

If you have expensive belongings like a high-end bicycle or nice laptop, it's worth making sure that your single-item coverage for insurance is enough to cover those items. If your *purr* item coverage is too low, you will be on the hook for the dif*fur*ence. A $3,000 computer might only have $1,000 of coverage if your *purr* item limit is low.

Renter's insurance protects you if everything out of your apartment gets stolen or burns up - many people think that their landlord's insurance will cover them in that case, but it does not. Legally, insurance can only cover the "interested party" (this one of the many reasons why you can't take out insurance on a rich neighbor's place and then burn it down). Renter's insurance helps protects you from the big unexpected disasters that would be a huge hit to your emergency fund. Renter's insurance usually quite inexpensive - around $10 or $15 each month - and is especially helpful if you're living on a low income and don't have a lot of savings yet. It's easy to get, too.

One last thing to look for on your homeowner and renter's insurance policies is to check if some of your property - say your computer or camera - is considered business equipment.

If you have a side-hustle or full-time job out of your home that you claim business deductions for on your taxes, that property may not be covered under your rental or homeowner insurance policy because it's considered the business's property. You may need to purchase a "rider" (an extra policy on top of your regular policy) or separate business insurance. Depending on the type of business you have, this could be very inexpensive. If you depend on your business equipment for your income, usually business insurance is worth having (it also can potentially protect you in the case of customer lawsuits). You may even be required to have business insurance in your jurisdiction in order to operate legally.

Business insurance is more complicated than the scope of this book, but that's where having a trustworthy insurance agent who understands your business is worth their weight in gold. Ask around for recommendations from colleagues in the same line of work - don't just pick the nice person you know from soccer games or the cat cafe - because insurance agents cycle in and out of the industry quickly and it's worth it to have an agent that understands your line of work. You can also check ohmydollar.com for a list of *purr*viders we trust.

Health Insurance

Health insurance is one of the most important things you can prioritize in your budget if you live in the United States. There's a lot of politics wrapped up in American health care and the specifics may be very different two weeks after I publish this book, so I'm only going to cover the broad strokes for you.

Furst: health insurance should be a priority for you. Remember how I was saying that your goal is to have insurance for the big, expensive things, and self-insure for the little things? The goal is to get your savings to a point where you've got the cash in your pocket to cover the little things, but that a big unexpected event that's beyond the scope of your emergency fund is covered.

If you've been to the hospital in America before, you might know that health care can be *paw*tentionally expensive. You get home from the doctor and there's not just one bill, there's stacks upon stacks of envelopes - from everyone in a lab coat who so much as glanced at you while you were at the doctor's office.

The thing about great health, is for nearly everyone, it's temporary. Our human bodies are fragile, and we have better and better technology to fix them, but you're playing a risky game if you try to pretend that you're going to be in perfect health and you don't need back up for an unexpected event. You can't predict the future and know that you will not break a bone or get hit with a big, expensive diagnosis or end up with a complicated pregnancy. Can you cover $1,000,000 out of pocket? I can't, and that's why I have health insurance.

Whatever you feel about America's complicated system of health care - which is far from perfect - we still want to get you to the point where you qualify for, can afford, and have budgeted for health insurance. I want you to be financially well, and that includes the resources to be physically well, as much as your body allows. Health insurance is a complicated and often discouraging maze, but it helps to remember, though, this is an open book test. This book is only scratching the surface but you can ask for help when you're navigating health care.

One thing you should understand about health insurance is that you need to be prepared early - usually you can't opt-out of coverage to save money and then join if you get hurt or sick. Health insurance requires you to opt-in during what is called the "open enrollment period" - which is usually a few months a year, usually in the fall or the beginning of the year - or if you have "special change of circumstance" - which is usually losing insurance (like if you lose a job), getting married, or having or adopting a child. Once you qualify, don't delay just to save a buck, because an unexpected health event can bankrupt you.

The majority of people in the US that have health insurance coverage get it through their employer. You often have no choice in what type of insurance you get when you get it through your employer, but you may get to choose your level of deductible and your share of the premium. Your premium is what you will pay - usually monthly, but possibly more frequently depending on your pay cycle - regardless if you use your health insurance. If you get your health insurance through your employer, they may cover all or most of your insurance premium.

In determining which plan to choose, understanding your own level of risk and your own health needs are helpful. You can run a simple break-even analysis on your deductible vs premiums. It's not as scary as it sounds. If you have a $1,000 deductible that means that you are going to need to cover your medical costs until you hit $1,000 total paid for the year, after which the insurance company will cover part of the cost.

There are certain preventative things - such as reproductive exams and annual check-ups - that are often covered in full even if you haven't met your deductible yet. This is where checking out the insurance packet or website is helpful, because you might owe nothing for certain types of appointments or medications even if you haven't hit your deductible yet.

Once you hit your deductible, your insurer will start paying part for your medical expenses for most everything. These will have a co-pay or co-insurance, which is the portion that you will be expected to cover. Co-pay is generally a fixed amount - such as a $25 fee for a specialist visit. Co-insurance is a percentage. Often this will be something like 80/20 which means 20% of the cost will be owed by you, and 80% will be covered by the insurance.

Usually there is a family deductible and an individual deductible on your health insurance plan. This is meant to prevent families from going broke paying for each person's health insurance deductible. Each family member will be covered if they reach their own individual deductible, but if the higher family deductible is met collectively, health plan benefits kick in for *every member* of the family whether or not they've met their own individual deductibles.

If one person in the family has high cost health needs, the family deductible can often make combining plans more affordable, even if there are higher premiums.

High Deductible and Health Savings Accounts

Just like with other types of insurance, a higher deductible means lower premiums. A high-deductible plans makes sense for two categories of people: really healthy people and folks with expensive health conditions. Really healthy people will pay less out of pocket, and will use their emergency fund to meet their deductible if they get injured or sick suddenly, but will save more month-to-month because they don't need coverage for everyday things.

Meanwhile, if you have cancer, arthritis, diabetes, or any other condition where management of the disease is quite expensive, it's likely you'll hit your deductible quickly, and a high-deductible plan with a health savings account could reduce your overall expenses because you will pay less overall between your premiums and co-pays. This is where running the numbers is helpful and your specific situation will vary.

If you have a high-deductible plan (as defined by law), there is a special type of savings account you can use for medical expenses. Health Savings Accounts (HSA) let you save pre-tax money - meaning you save more dollars without "feeling it" in your paycheck - to pay your expenses before you hit your deductible. That means you can save about $750 of your dollars to pay $1,000 of medical expenses (if your tax bracket is 25%).

These accounts are particularly great because they are simply a special savings account, so if you don't have any medical costs in a given year, a HSA acts a special medical emergency fund. Once you hit retirement age, a HSA will let you pull out money for any expense at all, so even if you're healthy, these accounts are great way to save some money and reduce the amount of taxes you pay.

Out of Pocket Maximum

One of the most important things to know about your insurance is your out-of-pocket maximum, or your stop-loss amount. This is the maximum you will pay in a given year. On many high-deductible plans, the out-of-pocket maximum is close to the deductible cost. Out-of-pocket maximums are the point at which the insurance company will cover 100% of medical costs after that amount - mine, for example, is $7,150 a year. This is good to know because having that number available in an emergency fund helps you reduce your chances of medical bankruptcy in the case of a very big expensive injury or illness. Most plans have a combined family out-of-pocket maximum as well as an individual one.

A "cap" on insurance used to be common but they were eliminated on most plans due to federal regulation. A cap is a limit on what the insurance would pay total for your care (either in your lifetime or in a year). A common cap was $1,000,000. Whenever possible, you want to have no cap, because if you get a triple bypass or chemotherapy, those bills can total well beyond a million. Ideally, you want to have both an out-of-pocket maximum that is affordable to you, and no cap in the case of something very expensive.

How to Get Insurance On Your Own

If you don't get health insurance through your employer, depending on your income and your state, you can get health insurance either through a state Medicaid program - this is if you fall below a certain income, right now in Oregon it is $17,000 for a single person with no kids - which will be free or extremely low-cost to you.

If your state doesn't have Medicaid available for your income, or if your income is too high, you can get health insurance through the marketplace. This is under constant flux due to changes in congress, so you can always check in with the Oh My Dollar! podcast for the latest info. The most important thing to know is that if you are median-income, you will get a tax credit that you can take monthly - or annually - to lower the monthly cost of your premium. Often the sticker price for insurance will not be what you pay, so don't get too scared away!

In every US state, if you're confronted with needing to buy insurance on your own and you simply cannot figure out which plan to get, you can get a health navigator - a licensed health insurance broker - at no cost to you. Health navigators are held to a legal standard where they must work in your best interest, and a good one will walk you through the different options with good explanations. Health insurance navigators are particularly helpful if you have a high-cost medication or potentially complicated health condition and need to know what your out of pocket costs will be on particular plans, or if a specialty provider will be covered.

For example, I have rheumatoid arthritis, so I need to make sure that my Rheumatologist is covered by a particular health insurance plan. I also need to check something called the formulary, which is the list of drugs that an insurance company will cover. For certain drugs, some insurers will cover only a small amount of costs before deductible. My speciality medication costs $6,000 a month out of pocket (yes, you see why I need insurance) so I need to check the that it is covered, and I need to check the cost of my co-pay with various health insurance plans. You'll be a smart kitten if you research this ahead of enrolling if you're buying your own insurance or have multiple choices at your employer, so that you can plan your budget around these costs.

Josy, Lover of Dogs and Kitties
Canada

DISABILITY INSURANCE

Disability insurance is designed to help you replace income if you become injured or sick and cannot work. Many people think that worker's comp will cover them, but the majority of disability claims are due to illness, not injury, and worker's comp only covers injury or illness that occured on the job. You won't get covered by worker's comp if you have cancer treatments or if you break your leg at your own home and can't work.

Your employer may provide private disability insurance that covers you. You want to make sure that the insurance they provide is long-term as well as short-term. Short-term insurance can be helpful (and is actually one of the main forms of paid maternity leave in the US), but your emergency fund, once it is in place, will cover most short-term disabilities. But long-term disability insurance is essential for most people that are not independently wealthy. It will help replace your lost income if you cannot go back to work. There's two terms you need to know when you're looking for disability insurance: elimination period and term.

The elimination period is the time before the insurance company will wait before they pay out after you are disabled. The longer your elimination period, the lower your premium cost. I recommend going for 180 days - six months - to lower your premiums. That will mean that you need to cover your own expenses out of savings for six months if you get sick or injured, before disability insurance will start paying you.

Usually disability insurance will pay a percentage of your income - fifty to sixty percent is usual - which means you'll need to be able to survive on that much while you find a new plan or until you are approved for social security as a supplemental income. Disability insurance income is tax free, though, which means it can "feel" like your job income did after taxes.

You ideally want ***own-occupation coverage,*** which will pay disability if you are not able to work in the job you trained in. So if your job is doing voiceover announcements, if you lose your voice permanently, own-occupation disability insurance would cover you even if you were able to work in another profession, since you would have to retrain and qualify for a new job that doesn't involve your voice.

The term of your disability insurance is how long it will pay out - the longer the term, the more expensive the insurance premium is - you can get coverage for 1 year, 5 years, 10 years, or until retirement age (when social security or retirement savings would start). I recommend 5 years or more if you can afford it, since it can take years to retrain for a new profession or to qualify for permanent disability through social security.

LIFE INSURANCE

There's a few things to know about life insurance: you don't need life insurance forever if you're building wealth, life insurance is not an investment vehicle and if you don't think about life insurance until you need it, it's too late.

Life insurance is primarily two types: whole life insurance and term. Term life insurance runs out after a set amount of time. If you keep working on your financial wellness, you will get to the point where your income from your investments in your retirement accounts will cover your expenses - particularly if you don't hold any debt. At that point, you're self-insured. In this case, you want to get term life insurance to cover you while you're young and healthy and easy to insure and while you're still in the "wealth building" stage of your financial plan. If you wait until you are sick, it is too late to get insurance.

Many middle class folks get trapped into "whole life" insurance policies. These policies mix together investments and insurance. They're also extremely profitable for life insurance agents to sell, so they're often what gets recommended if you go to an agent without doing any research beforehand.

In the investing chapter we learned that you want diversity in your investment portfolio to spread out the risk. Whole life insurance policies have you investing in a single company's stocks, and their returns are usually pretty terrible compared to what you could get in the stock market as a whole. What's more, if you die, these insurance policies "keep" the cash value they otherwise claim to be investing for you. They're also much much more expensive than term policies, often as much at five times more expensive. If you took the difference between a whole life policy and a term policy, you could save that money and invest it in your own retirement account, which your spouse or dependents can keep if you die. See why whole life is rarely a good deal?

Instead of a whole life insurance policy, you want to cover your lost income in the event of your death for your dependents - including your spouse or partner if you have one - with a relatively inexpensive term life insurance policy. The earlier you get this, the cheaper it is. Remember, it's just covering you in the first part of your working career - into your 50's - at which point, the aim is for your own assets to self-insure, because your dependents will be able to live off the wealth you've accumulated.

The rule of thumb is you want ten times your income- so if you make $40,000, you want $400,000 worth of coverage, which means that your beneficiaries will be able to get $400,000, which they can invest and pull out close to the equivalent of your salary each year after you pass.

If you are trying to figure out how much to cover a stay at home partner - remember that all work still has economic value, and you want to cover the cost of replacing their labor. If that person does childcare, you need to cover the cost of a nanny if they were to pass, so that's their "income".

For children, you only need to insure the cost of their funeral, unless they are a child starlet and are making money for the family. If you have an emergency fund in place you do not need insurance to pay for their funeral.

If you have no dependents or partner, you can go without life insurance, as long as you have the funds in place to cover a funeral. If you've got an emergency fund, then you're fine. Make sure, however, you have a living will in place regardless. There are some resources for planning that in the appendix (your "Hit By A Bus" folder.)

Hopefully you feel better prepared to get yourself insured! When considering insurance, remember that you are covering the essentials and the big downpours - don't fall into traps of covering things you can cover out of your own pocket, like a plane ticket insurance or jewelry loss or a cell phone. Insurance is generally logical if you could not cover the loss yourself, and if the event (death, disability, car crash) would be life-altering.

Discussion Questions

*These discussion questions are great if you are going through **A Cat's Guide to Money** with friends - but they're also worth having the conversation with yourself, your accountability partner, or just writing them out below.*

Many people put off getting insurance because they don't feel that they can afford it. Why do you think prioritizing the right types of insurance is important even when money is tight?

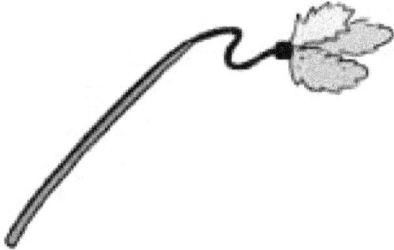

Talk about the difference between things that insurance covers and things that emergency funds cover.

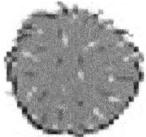

If you get term life insurance, the life insurance will end at some point compared to a whole life policy. Why would it make sense to get cheaper term life insurance policy instead of whole life policy then?

Week eight Action items

Audit your insurance coverage

Review your insurance coverage this week - do you have the essentials covered? Are you meeting the guidelines in this chapter? If you have your emergency fund in place, investigate a break-even analysis if you'd like to save money on premiums.

Start your "Hit By a Bus" folder

Talking about and thinking about death is hard for many people. But you can give a great gift to your loved ones if you organize your financial accounts and passwords for your death. Review the "Hit By a Bus" worksheet in the Appendix and get started on a single place to store everything your loved ones would need to know if you got gravely injured or died.

Insurance Coverage List

Insurance should be a purriority for your financial plan, especially if you are still paying off debt. Keep a list of your insurance coverage so you know where to find it in case of an emergency!

INSURANCE	PLAN #	COVERAGE AMOUNT	AGENT CONTACT	PREMIUM

Insurance to get

INSURANCE	DEADLINE TO GET
Health Insurance	
Term Life Insurance	
Renter's Insurance	
Homeowner's Insurance	
Auto Insurance	
Long-Term Disability Insurance	
Business Insurance	

You're PAWSOME!

Together, we've been through a lot of dif*fur*ent lessons over the past eight weeks, and you might be overwhelmed. But the good *mews* is that this is just the beginning!

Getting your money together is not a single event, it is a process. There's no trophy you can put on your shelf with a plaque that says "April 18th, 2018 - the Day I Got My Money Together."

You're going to have money (and life) stumbles, and I guarantee there is going to be hard work ahead of you. But now you have started the process by picking up this book and asking for help. And you're already better equipped to handle those money stumbles in the future than you were just a few weeks ago.

This book isn't comprehensive. In two hundred cat-filled pages I can't cover every change in the tax code, mortgage structure, or family money conflict. But I aim to give you a good structure to work from. If you take the principles in this book, one step at a time, and stay *meow*tivated, **you will find a since of calm about your money.**

These cats and worksheets will always be here whenever you need a little money support. I, and all 45 cats in this book, believe you can and will change your money story for the better.

There's no trophy for money meownagement, but there should be merit badges along the way

Some financial tasks are soul-sucking or boring.

Hopefully you can make them a little more fun by coloring in these merit badges for your money accomplishments!

www.ingramcontent.com/pod-product-compliance
Lightning Source LLC
Chambersburg PA
CBHW062101220526
45471CB00010B/3561